The Funeral Officiant

&

Ceremony

A Course
In Funeral
Celebrancy

CIPO/Sec.49and53
2020 copyright ®

Table of Contents

Chapter I

Page 11 ~ What is the Canadian Society Of Celebrants?
　　　　　Being a member of the CSOC

Page 12 ~ Curricula expectation

Page 13 ~ Certification/ Mentoring:
　　　　　What is a Certified Funeral Celebrant?

Page 14 ~ Key responsibility of A Celebrant/
　　　　　The Funeral Director's role

Page 15 ~ Why Have A Funeral Celebrant ?

Page 16 ~ The Funeral Home/Centre

Page 17 ~ The Mission

Page 18 ~ What are Celebrants? What is the Value ?

Page 19 ~ What is a Funeral ? The First Call

page 20 ~ First Call: How to deal with it & where to meet ?

Page 21 ~ When faced with the fact of a loss:

Page 22 ~ The snipping off effect
　　　　　Disbursements/Third party supplier(s)

Page 23 ~ There to perform a function or pay respects?

Page 24 ~ Bereavement is a process

The Funeral Officiant & Ceremony

Table of Contents

Chapter I

Page 25 ~ What is a Ceremony ?

Page 26 ~ Semi-Secular Vs. Secular

Page 27 ~ Secular and Non-Secular

Pages 28/9 ~ What really is the Funeral Experience ?
TRADITION

Page 30 ~ Death

Page 31 ~ IN MEMORY OF

Page 32 ~ The Sample Eulogy

Page 33 ~ 2nd Eulogy Sample

Pages 33-4 ~ Sept. 26th, 2018 Public speaking Sample for a pre-paid Funeral Service Ceremony…
Writing The Eulogy of Aunt Faye:

Page 35 ~ Preparing the Funeral Service Ceremony before a loved one dies.

Page 36-37 ~ Back to Writing The Eulogy For Aunt Faye

Pages 38&42-4 ~ May 23rd, 2019 Public speaking for a pre-need Funeral Service Ceremony

Pages 38-40 ~ Clergy Documents And Sample Sheets

Table of Contents

Chapter I

Page 41 ~ The Funeral Liturgy

Page 45 ~ Pre-need Vs. Pre-paid

Pages 45-9~ What is the relevance for a CONTRACT ?

Pages 49-56~ The significance of a Pre-Arrangement/Pre-plan?

Pages 57/8 ~ Metaphysical (Spiritual) Ministries, Pastoral and Funeral Ceremony Services

Pages 59-60 ~ Non-Denominational Vs. Multifaith

Page 61 ~ What are the Celebrant's Responsibilities?

Pages 61-68~ Atheist/Humanist and Civil Celebrants

Page 66 ~ What can be included in this fee?

Pages 68-70 ~ The Final Draft

Chapter II

Page 71 ~ Resistance/Trauma/Shock Different Types of Funeral Tributes

Page 72 ~ Eulogy/Tribute/building of a Portrait & Misconceptions

Pages 73-5 ~ The Eulogy & Ceremony Script

Page 76/7 ~ YOU GET WHAT YOU PAY FOR

Pages 78-81 ~ What type of Funeral Ceremony Service(s) do you prefer?

The Funeral Officiant & Ceremony

Table of Contents

Chapter II

Pages 81-6 ~ Interment/Green and Natural Burials

Page 86 ~ But what about Cremated Remains?

Page 87 ~ IS A Memorial Service The Same as A CELEBRATION OF LIFE?

Pages 87/8 ~ HOW DO YOU PLAN A CELEBRATION OF LIFE ?/A Celebration of Life service can include

Page 89 ~ Family/Client Decisions When planning for a Celebration of Life

Pages 90-/1 ~ Is a Bespoke Ceremony a Hybrid ?

Page 92 ~ Graveside Ceremony Service can provide/ Excerpt A brief Interview Case Scenario snippet!

Pages 93-9 ~ FUNERAL CEREMONY for Richard Johnson

Pages 100/1 ~ Elaborate and or Unusual Services

Pages 102-3 ~ A Memorial Ceremony/Memorials

Pages 104/5 ~ The Initial Call and The Interview Checklist

Chapter III

Page 105 ~ During The Interview: "Helping To Create a Portrait"

Pages 106-8 ~ The Interview Checklist/During the Initial Meeting

Pages 109-17~ Bereavement Initial Interview Checklist

Table of Contents

Chapter III

Pages 117/18 ~ During the initial meeting/Interview Checklist

Page 119 ~ Approving the Ceremony & Transcript Delivery

Pages 120-2 ~ Modification of the Ceremony Script

Pages 123-25 ~ What happens after the initial meeting? Music/ Other Speakers/ Suggested Readings

Pages 126-35 ~ MILITARY/ FALLEN FIREFIGHTERS & LAW ENFORCEMENT FUNERALS

Page 136 ~ A Moment Of Silence

Pages 137-42 ~ Traditional Symbols and Ceremony Elementals

Chapter IV

Page 143 ~ Sundries & Disbursements

Page 144 ~ Various Encounters

Pages 145/6 ~ What is Leadership

Pages 147/8 ~ Gaining Trust/How Much Can A Celebrant Charge ?/ Collaboration

Pages 149-52 ~ Pricing Samples

Page 153 ~ The Celebrant's Role/ Making Initial Contact

Pages 154/5 ~ Go deeper with compassion

Pages 155/6 ~ Offering Ceremony Suggestions

The Funeral Officiant & Ceremony
Table of Contents

Chapter IV

Pages 156/8 ~ Setting Service Elements in Order/ Memorials/Reflection Time

Pages 158-62 ~ Order of Ceremony

Pages 162-7 ~ The importance of: The Anatomy of A Ceremony !

Pages 168-70 ~ (Lest We Forget)Remembrance Day Order of (100th Commemorative)Ceremony

Chapter V

Pages 171/2 ~ Tragic Deaths

Pages 173/4 ~ Public Speaking and Officiating

Page 175 ~ Officiants/Celebrants

Pages 176-80~Setting the Tone within the opening of the Ceremony

Page 181 ~ Preparing the Eulogy

Pages 182/3 ~ Tributes & Readings/Summing Up/ Readings Prior to Committal

Page 184 ~ The Committal/The Committal Process/Closing Words

Page 185 ~ Benediction/

Page 186 ~ Ceremony for a Stillborn Baby

Pages 186-97 ~ FUNERAL CEREMONY for Charlotte Sky Ericson

Table of Contents

Chapter V

Pages 197-203 ~ To recap:

Chapter VI

Pages 203-5 ~ SELECTING FUNERAL SONGS

Pages 206-9 ~ After the Ceremony/ Advertising/Marketing

Pages 210/11 ~ To Further Elaborate

Pages 212/13 ~ Funeral Ceremony and Children

Pages 214-24 ~ FUNERAL CEREMONY(Client Copy) for Jessica's CAT GEMMA

Page 225 ~ Pet Funeral: Common Elements

Pages 226-28 ~ For your beloved Pet and Some Considerations A Generic Tribute as an Outline Guide

Page 229 ~ From Simple to Elaborate

Page 230 ~ Pre-planning

Chapter VII

Pages 231-246 ~ FUNERAL CEREMONY(Celebrant Copy) for John Smitty Smith

Page 247 ~ How To Write A Funeral Program

Pages 248-51 ~ Prayers/poems/excerpt reads&quote samples

The Funeral Officiant & Ceremony
Table of Contents

Chapter VII

<u>Pages 252-55</u> ~ <u>For Annual Licensing Renewal Professionals</u>

Chapter VIII

<u>Pages 256-58</u> ~ <u>WHERE DO WE GO FROM HERE</u> ?

PURPOSE

The principles and practice of Funeral Ceremony presents to the Celebrant/Officiant and closely allied professions a dignified involvement of modern Funeral rites; to include constructive guidance for the bereaved to follow through the grieving process. The Funeral Director too can benefit from this, in their local public relations program.

This book can add great value for the bereaved and their contemporaries' attitudes toward grief and help to resolve unexpressed behaviours within the family dynamic, community and society. The text is designed as a continuing reference; it can be an excellent source for public relations and the respect you seek from the realization of its importance. Canadian Society Of Celebrants motto: is to bring together the "<u>B.E.S.T.</u>" forward !

Business

Education

Spirituality

Training

PREFACE

Make no mistake; that for this book exclusively;
the capitalization of certain words(within these following 248 pages to come); they have been placed there, meticulously and with purpose. Titles of authority such as "Ceremony", "Celebrant/Officiant", "Clergy" and even "Coroner"; they are going to be relevant to thread(into the psyche) a common element, on the level of respect and that otherwise would not be there in common English literature. The book aims to teach the student respect; however not a requirement for any other purpose to uphold and that of common practice.

Volume One will hopefully ingrain this unique "*que tu sais quoi*" quality level of understanding(in reference to specific things, places and other such social values) to experience and that will not be necessary in Volume Two.

NOTE:

AVAILABLE IN E-BOOK FORMAT

ISBN: 9781777104108

The Funeral Officiant & Ceremony : A Course In Funeral Celebrancy ~CSOC volume ONE

ELECTRONIC FORMAT INCLUDES an additional 12 page "PET MEMORIAL AND TRIBUTE" PACKAGE SAMPLE

Chapter I

What is the Canadian Society Of Celebrants?

The vision: A collaboration with other like minded entrepreneurs to form a mentoring incentive from the educational body of CSOC. To build and provide programs that can bring about more Celebrants and Ceremony Officiants.

The mission: From a spiritual perspective, open to serve all faiths and interdependently thriving. To provide a curricula through self study books; such as this one and an online presence, that can assist in certifiable courses toward a diploma. Canadian Society Of Celebrants aims to further enhance the theoretical, with a mentorship practical component from other like minded online portal members, in Canadian Celebrant training.

Being a member of the CSOC:

Canadian Society Of Celebrants is not a licensing providing body; as of yet, there has been no regulated requirements set in place for Celebrants to carry a licence. The CSOC is a legal corporate entity and should the need arise for such standards to be in place; it will aspire the CSOC and its members by offering this option. Upon certification from the CSOC the initiation into the CSOC begins. You can then become a member and for a yearly fee be kept on file as an active participant. As members the aim is to bring together education with business, by training and hiring. A healthy record keeping and reporting incentive is our mission; the amount said Ceremonial/Life Celebrations (as per pending qualifications); that on occasion from this list will be asked to mentor and/or perform such said qualified duties. Also, there is no stipulation that states a member of such standing cannot be ordained as a Minister or have any pastoral affiliations(as well as licensing)outside of CSOC. All are welcomed inclusively to join in...

Curricula expectation :

This book will be the first volume and curriculum of its kind; toward a "Family&Funeral Celebrant" diploma.
The book is exclusively adjusted for the required Funeral Celebrancy certification. The curricula will start the reader on an independent study path, and stands as a timeless potential for many other probabilities to be made possible.
Online tutoring feedback and a one, on one mentoring can take place, however optional. Feedback on assessed work is only optional for portal members and further advice to better guide improving on performance. An online course will also give this book for an opportunity and/or just directly through electronic feedback; for written commentaries and individual discussions. These options are the tools that will be made use of via e-mail/or on line project(s); quiz(s) and finally a certification. This book is the hard copy; however any other correspondence can be made upon proper payment to request further learning: of your own completed script and payment per assessment script. This designed structure is to help accommodate for those who might not be able to invest the time and/or money right away and/or all at once. As things continuously unfold for us; it is an ongoing process that will require from our own life path destiny and as the reader wishes to progress; from their own authentic timetable. Dive into it as deep as you are willing and with small increments at a time.
We all have our own divine timing and as we work through the surface of life begin to become accepting more and more of this depth we call awareness.

By purchase of this book your enrolment has commenced..

Bravo !

The Funeral Officiant & Ceremony

Certification:

* You will be asked for a copy of a Ceremony script; this will be of a Ceremony you perform(Ceremony Script will be modified, that your clients identities can be protected).

* Must video tape the performance as a rehearsal run prior to the actual Ceremony and submit along with the above script for further feed back on your practice and monitoring quality.

Mentoring:

A qualified person that you can choose to shadow over with and likewise they can help by showing up for your first Ceremony. This is the way to get the proper feedback on your practice; the experience that will help build your confidence and as clientele as well. This is a prerequisite for a diploma; however other arrangements can be made adaptable and open to negotiate a fee, for an actual CSOC mentor ...

What is a Certified Funeral Celebrant?

Trained and certified to provide a Funeral, Memorial or Celebration of Life services. These services are highly personalized Ceremonies; designed to reflect the personality, lifestyle and beliefs of the person and or animal who died. We are here to encourage participation by family and friends to also co-create into a meaningful event.
We are responsible in writing the script for the entirety of the performance and assist with the facilitating process to direct and guide the Ceremony along from beginning to the end.

Key responsibility of A Celebrant:

- Meet with the family and methodically record details from the decedent's life.
- What you write down must depict the true character of that person
- By sitting down with the bereaved family and/or friends, you will put together an outline of the Ceremony.
- The outline of the Ceremony is the creation of his/her it(loved pet) portrait.
- A Bespoke Ceremony, properly prepared, can then be delivered with confidence, care and sensitivity.
- The Aim is to help the family and other mourners who are coming to terms with their loved one's death..
- For a Funeral service you have a window of preparing the Ceremony(3-5)days?

The Funeral Director's role:

Kindness and just like a warm smile it can become contagious. Although the "Funeral Director's role" is to arrange the service, and not by any means to support the Celebrant (one day this can change). For now all we can do is reach out for the collaboration as much as possible. Show them you appreciate their team work and learn how you can become a team player.

In conjunction with the many venues and the staff that they provide; the Funeral Director is in charge of certain things you might require, such as: an operative microphone and/or other preparations for the Ceremony. It is just not just about the Funeral Director having to get to know what it means to be a Celebrant to enhance this relationship it is best to know the Funeral professions side of things as well.

The Funeral Officiant & Ceremony

Why Have A Funeral Celebrant ?

Mourners did not ask for such circumstances and most of the time do not want to know about how to learn to let things go.
A Celebrant can be supportive to help guide; advise along the process and through creative expression for a scripted Ceremony. These special moments, anecdotes and other snippets of time to share while writing down a eulogy. A growing number of individuals call themselves non-religious and do not participate with a faith community. Also, many people follow a strong spiritual path; but are not religious. For both groups, when someone dies, they are often unclear about how to design a tribute that is best fitting. Friends and family often want to participate in the creation and presentation of a personalized gathering; but may be uncomfortable, or unable to speak publicly about death and the loss of a loved one. Funeral Celebrants support the individual or family decision to present in this way a spiritual gathering. CSOC follows a strong spiritual path rather and is safe to say "non-religious".
It will accentuate the multi-faith and intercultural expressions to aspire with "Semi-Secular" and other such non-denominational groupings. CSOC can and will adapt religious ideas to recreate and co-create with collaboration from other Religious Officials and/or likewise independently bespoke a meaningful scripted Ceremony. This given knowledge is what stands out mostly from the CSOC over any other Celebrancy organizations and Celebrant foundations.
With CSOC, we want families to know one thing; our strength in this thing called "imagination". With imagination "the sky is the limit" ! The Ceremony is personalized to reflect your loved ones lifestyle and personality.

FUNERAL CELEBRANTS
                        are becoming a popular choice in Canada !

The Funeral Home/Centre:

Once upon a time in the province of Ontario Canada; Funeral homes were kept separated from the business of Cemeteries and their day to day operations. In 2002 this idea started changing and alliances were formed and grew.

Most of the "mom & pop" Funeral homes and their chapels were taken over by corporations. The cemeteries were centres but not actual Funeral homes. When the two of them did merge; another entity became apparent. Bereavement centres can one day perhaps envision to accommodate for all, and depending on the licence held, the services that they can be providing.

These pleasant surroundings that can best accommodate for all families, hold a high level of servitude cultural and religious needs of each service rendered. One day perhaps and unlike any other Celebrating Ministries; the Celebrant might be of its own body to uphold a licence; and/or licensed under the same body as the Funeral Director; to provide these kind of services and meet on equal footing; with all the other licensing staff, and that does include religious Clergy affiliates. For now however they are obligated not so much for these kind of services but can however professionally provide their clients with easy-to-use, member designed website portals and is another way of expressing your condolences. User-friendly online resource centres can be very helpful to starting a personalized online Memorial/condolence; however not to the extent of Ceremony/Celebrant Officiant services to connect with. These referrals must be sought out independently by those in need of such services.

Memorial services and the Celebration of Life are not often promoted; because there is no reason to cater in these Funeral homes/centres/chapels. When Funeral Centres do provide these services, family members were already buried, or have had their cremated remains scattered there. Other social clubs and unrelated venues to Funeral establishments have and do provide the indoor space of encouragement.

The Funeral Officiant & Ceremony

The Mission:

To establish and support a relevant relationship of transparency and integrated truth; that can provide an equal footing, between the Celebrant and Funeral Director. Until that day they can be merged into one; the reverence must be included just the same as one would with: an Embalmer- an Arranger and Director as well as Pre-Arranger and Sales Associate. All the many roles that from these facets they do make a Class-1 Funeral Director and in the province given as the example of Ontario. There are the few obvious ways to hire for these Celebrancy services?

In future perhaps some negotiating can be made for us as Celebrants to be contacted directly through the Funeral Director. Since anyone can perform this type of Ceremony; to have the decedent's body present does limit where the service can be held. Wouldn't it be great for the Funeral parlour to work as in partnership with the Celebrant? Better yet for the Funeral directing staff to be qualified enough to officiate the Ceremony?

Perhaps the Ceremony script can be time consuming and require the Celebrant to write it out and then have one of the Funeral staff officiate. After all, Funeral Directors day to day involvements are all about team work experience and much value for all of their accomplishments. The other option has been applicable thus far and mostly for the Celebrant to be the 3rd party, and as an outsider to be welcomed in by the client/family. The family would let the Funeral Director know their interest to invest in you specifically; as the Celebrant and then this way, having to make contact for the relevant arrangements(might also organize an Honorarium). Alternatively the client/family, can make the arrangements directly with the Celebrant.

What are Celebrants?

Focused individuals and/or a grouping of practicing ceremony professionals(in some cases hold council for licensing), with a common intent of bringing folk together, for a special occasion. Ceremony Officiants: are passionate writers/speakers; with their advice and direction, a space can be held for praise worthy events to take place.

What is the Value ?

The deceased, he/she/it(your pet) had a name:
The acknowledgement is in the details of this shared camaraderie for the deceased. By creating a space for sympathetic expression; it can start with the sharing of as simple written, carefully thought out message and as one would, with condolences. These encouraging words of hope, or a positive wish for the bereaved. The specific qualities and favourite memories; they remind us all to be strong and keep authentic. This is the best kind of support that can empower the bereaved; rather than having them rely or depend on certain individuals, that have a special bond with to be able to pinpoint the best activity for you to suggest. Offering to reach out in this way provides a creative openness to share the grief alongside the bereaved. The opportunity for as many to become involved in this experience can be of a reprieve between all who come together; no matter who or what the decedent was to, or for them; their loving and sincere remarks will and can add to these memories a value. Again we can help to advise with honesty and awareness what they can expect; however must prepare ourselves as their only back up for just in case they cannot make it to the podium to speak...All are invited to stand up and speak their piece however not required. Children can also have their place where they can ask as many questions and in this script perhaps be included the opportunity; however never forced.

This is where you as the Officiant can improvise the script and even speak on their behalf.

The Funeral Officiant & Ceremony

What is a Funeral ?

Often the initial step toward separation from the decedent and the beginning of the grief process. It declares a death has occurred; this social gathering aspect psychologically begins for the first step in healing. The Funeral ritual makes the death a reality for those who are bereaved. The ritual can include the viewing of the deceased as the harsh reality that they are to confirm for the persons grieving of this death. Embalming will provide the safest opportunity to give back this memory; with great reverence and dignity of how they wish to be remembered. This is the time for telling stories and sharing memories; as well as performing rituals to help release the many blockages from mourning this loss and holding back expression, in a supportive space, that can encourage reintegration. The Funeral gives structure for the proper interaction to take place; the space and time allotted to attend that can reaffirm the importance of living once we say goodbye.

Preparing the Ceremony(3-5)days?

First Call: How to deal with it ..And where to meet ?

Take down the address and their telephone number; where they can be reached.. as well as email addresses and other such online devices that the other members can attend; but cannot actually make it physically to be present, for the interview. Ask the caller to bring as many family members that would wish to be involved; any additional written condolences; music, songs, poetry, religious or non religious readings and excerpts they or anyone else who wishes to contribute; as well as photo albums or most recent picture that they will be Memorializing on the day of...

ACIFC CSOC

First Call: how to deal with it ..And where to meet ?

This word originated from the idea of a Funeral home(back in the day)receiving their "First Call" and to establish if it was an at need or a preened: For the purpose of our mission and this book; only the relevant we will make use of to appear and for the reader to create their own.

Informant: _____ Relationship: _____ .

Beneficiary's(the decedent's)full name _____ ?

Was the Ceremony arranged in advance?   Yes or No

Have we served them before ?

What kind of service are they looking for ?

(Time availability ?)This will be the big give away; because for an actual Funeral service the time is limited and with regards to preparing a full-on Ceremony 3-5 days !

Is it going to include a Burial; Cremation or Cemetery service?

Where and when is the service and/or are the services to be held?

Are they the purchaser of the Funeral service ?

Are they the ones who will be in charge of paying us for these services ?

Where and when would they like to meet for an initial interview check list and taking down of information ?

The Funeral Officiant & Ceremony

<u>When faced with the fact of a loss:</u>

It is important to recognize that Funerals are for the living…
For those who will suffer the trauma of losing a loved one.
It is through the Funeral process that a number of emotional needs are met for those who grieve. A Funeral is similar to other Ceremonies in our lives. Like a graduation Ceremony, a Wedding, and/or a Baptism; a Funeral is a rite of passage by which we recognize an important event that distinguishes our lives. Re-establishing a place in our community without the loved one.

Knowing how to switch on and off from one role to another is one thing and merging them all is another. This piece of wisdom is as important as knowing each role so very well as to have the confidence to play them. When merging from one task to another is what is simultaneously considered as going with the flow. When allowing every moment to flow through us energetically, otherwise the impossible resistance will and can exhaust into a powerless struggle to commit for any task. The harmony of every aspect must be at the very least respected and by becoming more aware; the synchronistic collaboration of its very co-creative possibilities to comprehend. To trust in this resonance and to respond from each and every moment as tapped in and turned on, well that is the greatest value in the many aspects that is team work. Remember that the Funeral Director used to be at one time or another and not too very long ago; they used to be the ones responsible for bringing it all together.

The snipping off effect:

Now more than ever before; to disconnect one part of itself in favour of another, might be clever, but also very dangerous. Switching off and compartmentalizing is not really teamwork; however very much a disconnect, that would be adding more stress fractures of competition and remorse from power struggles. Make certain that these convictions of convenience to connect or disconnect become reintegrated and recapitulated to once again accomplish what it means, to actually be a Funeral Director. The only way to be able to accomplish such a task; is by giving it awareness and not to close off from it. This book might help to focus on the inclusiveness rather than the exclusiveness of the Funeral and grieving process, that does also include the

<u>"Funeral Celebrant"</u>. The mission is to bring about unity peace and ease from previous resistance of dis-alignment and disharmony.

Disbursements/Third party supplier(s):

Other such sundries will further be explored throughout the book and given independently under such titles as to the benefits of contract and pre-arrangements. It is wise however to consider from the Funeral profession's side; how we might be included and perceived as Celebrants. When we are placed under this category and in some cases the contract from the Funeral business, can include an Honorarium (anything under this title is not added to for any further taxes). Most of the time the purchaser will initialize these kind of products and services. This kind of acknowledgement is a formal agreement between the purchaser and Funeral establishment, as their agent to obtain our services. In this case our clients must be aware and that unless other arrangements can be made with the Funeral Director, the purchaser(our potential client) will be held liable to pay us directly and will agree to save the Funeral Director from any said claims to pay us (Honorarium) our stipend fee.

The Funeral Officiant & Ceremony

There to perform a function or pay respects?

How do we not draw attention in our unwillingness to participate ? With these Ceremonies there is no enforceable code to obey or be cast out. This is an etiquette that will honour all participants and in their own authentic reverence to hold the space, just by being present. In most cases Funeral Directors have been known to get fired over these ridiculous inactions(disobedience with ridicule and taken as an insult); just for not personally partaking in the ritual that would require such things as: the eating of their client's food and/or hand gesturing of a cross over their body. This questions the very meaning of crossing the line and as a professional the very fabric that must be held firm with these boundaries; especially when met with such rigid standards. As a professional you must know from the very beginning to stand your ground in the role you play and function that you provide no matter what. Otherwise you will be led along unwillingly by the Pastor or any other Religious Official that you must co-operate alongside with. Or the refusal to perform such said "Semi-Secular" Ceremonies. In this case the pressure to become more than a Celebrant might be the case for further growth into your very own and will not be asked of such said demands from others in this way again. Be it a Celebrant, a Religious Official, a Funeral Director, or just a layperson there for the experience, you are not there to simply follow along(unless you want to).

Bereavement is a process:

It can be a fine line that does get blurry from empathy to sympathy and likewise the observer and observed. We don't have to give permission for others to trample over &the how we must participate in the negotiating factor, that reinforces other than our own agendas. Ultimately the authority is given off collectively by its investors. When we allow others to exploit our heart, what else is left ? This book is for the novice who wishes to take their power back. By creating your very own meaningful gathering and Ceremony; specifically designed around death and bereavement. It will not require the authorization of any kind, to profit from your heart's intentions. How would you like to know more about these services and specifically designed with this in mind? Connection will become empowerment when we can lift the many veils of secrecy. The options made available throughout the grieving process and along the way, the many kinds of Ceremony; that can be expressed for the experience through spiritual creative consciousness.

The cost cannot really be compared when it comes to the actual Funeral service with the decedent present and then later be expressed again in a Memorial or Celebration of Life Tribute. It's all about how much time is spent in the actual preparation and likewise the actual event given to present itself in the actual Ceremony. This is why it is important to go over packages and price lists; however all across the board a stipend fee might be considered as an Honorarium(for each Ceremony performed; as in the case of the actual Funeral there can be more than one to complete the service with). Accepting the alchemical process from the physical into the metaphysical.

Admittedly when this happens; the entire service becomes a memory and that revolves all around the "Fun" "we shared together". In this love that teaches us to break free from its conditions and with it explore the possibilities with others to transcend from the pain as a Memorial experience.

The Funeral Officiant & Ceremony

What is a Ceremony ?

These services can be basic to most elaborate, creative expressions of nature and in ritual design; inclusively and exclusively, for society and the individual. It will evoke the theosophical reflection, traditional life and personality affiliations, of those we serve.
For the purpose of this volume, the focus is on Funerals and exclusively that of Memorialization. In this case the reader can become empowered by its awareness and perhaps carry onto its connective course, that will provide certification... More importantly the know how from this book that will deliver to the reader much more confidence to participate in this kind of practice....The Celebrant does not have to be a licensed Religious Official nor a certified Celebrant with a diploma even; rather the value will become more apparent from this reading to experience and with further more practical applications if you will.
Secondly never assume how the Ceremony should or must take place; we are only the advisors and the pointers.
This is a collaboration, with you as the messenger and can likewise be given the option to co-create with the creator; as well as, to give the message out...The creative process, is encouraged for the family and that of the surviving members to express in any way, shape or form. We are there, as guides to make suggestions and assist in the direction of its process.
We are not the story makers, we are the gatherers, in helping to put it all together, piece by piece; all the many pieces to create a portrait; of who or what we gather, to place focus on and tribute for...Prepare to give meaning and that the right kind of relevance to your Ceremony or any other family's situation.
After all, there is nothing wrong with being well educated, is there ?

Semi-Secular Vs. Secular:

Many organizations are seeking to grasp in the multi-layered expression that can accept minor and major perspectives to be received with reverence. Western society continues to embrace the Eastern philosophies of Ceremony with much more relevance than ever before. Sometimes we can find the merging of a peanut butter cup and dipped into chocolate, to be divine; while others prefer a piece of chocolate dipped in peanut butter; rather feel the dissonance and keep them separate; preferring one over the other, as to go as far as to become exclusive in this preference. Such opinions become the systems of belief and with the passing of a loved one in this way. Although parables were greatly favoured with the one "Ascended Master"; the thought of having more than one might break the mould for something more…The exploration for expansion has broken many hearts and shattered the minds of many; however the healing from such grief has created a bigger space to love and know thyself much deeper than before. Could it be that a Non-Secular perspective is just the scratching at the surface of this, its very own psyche? Perhaps our Souls can recall these celebrations of "One's Life" and as threshold crossings, to remind us of this linear time existence.

The Funeral Officiant & Ceremony

Secular and Non-Secular :

Celebrants are not subject to any of the monastic confinements; nor does the word "Secularism" to suggest that we must be an Ethical Union of Humanist Societies. Celebrants can serve all walks of life including the Atheist(Non-Secular/Secular confused) Political "Mad Hatters" and Agnostics. On the other hand Canadian Society Of Celebrants, can incorporate much more meaningful "Secular" methods and Non-Secular beliefs; with the interfaith and all other such non-denominational ministry affiliations alike.
Thusly collaboration with a Religious Official/Funeral Director, as well as with immediate family and friends; co-operation is the key. Always know your place within the thick of it, your mission and the duties and obligations that have been asked from you by the decedent; the predeceased and likewise predecessoral agreements, past down through lineage and so on and so forth.
The mission of your engagement and the role you play in all of this; it must be well defined and given healthy boundaries to achieve. We are simple servants with less creative limitations to aspire unconditional self expression with. More will be explained in the next following chapters.

What really is the Funeral Experience ?

The moment all assisted life supports are stopped and/or from the moment a loved one stops breathing; this in itself begins the ritual. The Funeral experience is all about the decedent's transition and seeing to it that their wishes are received. All their requests, as the celebration will revolve around whatever theme the survivors had between them relative.
The send off is from that stationed point of reference; where the decedent uniquely had identified with and shared. From its ancestral communications passed along to the grieving survivors for interpretation and the ability to satisfy this connection. It is about finding just the right frequency with that familiar channel and through best fitting, a reconnect again ... Anything less of its vibration just won't do.
As it happens the Funeral service gets wrapped up pretty quickly; leaving very little time for emotional assessment. This is why it is encouraged to pre arrange these things completely; meaning Ceremony services as well, that can be of option to refine and rather than be done from scratch.
More will be discussed; including the option for Pet Memorials and other types of services without the body present and/or with your loved one's cremated remains. This is a process and on the journey less defined open to much hijacking from charitable organizations and the disguise paved with good intentions from volunteerism...Like any other traditional religious occultism and at the heart of all "Epitaphs"; "Memorial Tributes" the tugging of these guilt strings to gather and congregate in the very contrary impersonal participation. Spirituality does not have to become hijacked by previous recordings to form as structure to how the grieving process must occur.

The Funeral Officiant & Ceremony

<u>What really is the Funeral Experience</u> ?
Over and over again the same old variance with different by-laws to adhere to and protest in the giving back as testimonial enforcements. It is a very subjective mess and that can be left open to re-interpretation by those who might be more objective.
Where do we show compassion and when do we draw the line with charity ? Always reassure when dealing with the bereaved; that they are in good hands with the Funeral establishment and staff that they have chosen.

TRADITION:

The need for cultural identity has us promoting into certain tribes that can support us. This concept is made reference to and sometimes it could be viewed as a paradox when mentioning "traditional". For some it is the only cause for celebration and for others the agitation to reconfigure just the same; however it does have its level of importance to value. The very order to string along and carry out performance. Where does the marker go?
Where do we place the tomb stone/monument? Certain ground rule applications such as when carrying in your decedent loved one in and out of Church/Chapel service(feet first or head first) and right to burial where the trip-bar is the foot end to be placed and where the head for a ground burial. These are certain standards that have made their way from such customs mandatory in some cases and with others not so much adherence is required. Respecting through knowledge of these collective agreements, is a moral and ethical common courtesy. We all must start learning from somewhere and in this case synthetic ideas, are easier to grasp; than in their original raw state. Like any other invention, traditions take the lead in most of the adolescent training for a truly remarkable Celebrant.
Be open to the unknown, it is not a deviance; rather the unknowable experience of Ceremony, can and will better define you as brilliant as you are the "Guide". Know that everything always starts off as a preference in most cases with tradition.

Death:

"When the consciousness shuts off and the soul it leaves the body, what then"? Energy is never lost nor gained; rather transmuted into something else and likewise this consciousness can transcend to somewhere else.
From the moment someone dies, they become a memory; however it cannot all take place as quickly as the Funeral. This is a process that surviving members have to work through and unravel as their soul's adventure for expansion…
The celebration of a life might be one theme…
With the initial Ceremony it will begin the theme of letting go Ceremony service and will be all about accepting.

For the purpose of this book we must decide, what it is we want; by taking a look at what it means to empower and/or disable oneself and others. To depend on others is alright, just as long as these relationships empower; rather than disable.
When inequalities are met with more inequalities, a dysfunctional relationship between them will occur.
These relationships are codependent; where one must come out as losing for the other one to win. With death there already is a loss felt; this feeling of victimhood psychologically will attract and the enablement from its body of institutions, be it charitable or volunteer ? This book aims to please the giver and the receiver; so that both sides can benefit as equals.
Mastery is key component and for everyone to benefit that will present themselves the interest to learn. Learn how to be always a few steps ahead of what the co-creative process and with that of its collaborating parts. Know your place in within the mix of it and where do you stand in all of this? Ultimately, it is you who will be responsible for putting this together.

The Funeral Officiant & Ceremony

IN MEMORY OF:

Memorial services and Tributes, no matter how traditional or alternative; must be about the surviving members learning how to cope after the fact. In its truest sense the exchange of memories to share and resonate the many layers of its variations. At the heart of the entirety is the telling of a story; this story is all about our personal connection with the loss and everything relative from our own perspective. Great idea to gather in as many as can be added in this way from various perspectives and by combining of the many little references. These stories and by so many others told then will add to create the bigger much more meaningful picture.

This portrait is the image of the being who impressed upon our hearts this way and now are sitting over in the next room listening everything we have to say. Most of all feeling these shared circumstances with the others the deceased has touched.

Think of it as the last party with us we might ever have to have them witness in this body before it lays to rest. Perhaps there will be other times where we can come again to revisit these memories as we pay tribute and celebrate their life without their body present? Their likes and dislikes as well as any other commonalities and ties of these familiar connections we can all relate in our own special way. The way it activated our soul from special circumstances; these experiences that we hold so dear and in this way has connected us with others. As family, friends and other relations, relative that makes this tribe so special in the community and world wide…Decide what is your role you play in all of this from the very beginning; because chances are you will be called again and again to see it through to the very end. Although later in the book a few more structures with scenarios will be given; that can be made for study and to go through as you would be given from your own examples.

The following can be a warm up to what's to come:

The Sample Eulogy:

October 3rd, Thursday 2019.. Excerpt from Frank Clayton's Funeral service

Officiant: Surely goodness and mercy shall follow me all the days of my life and I shall dwell in the house of the Lord forever.

I understand that Frank's youngest daughter; Tracy would like to come up here and say a few words.

1st Eulogy

During his last few years, my father and I, have been on quite a journey together.
For years he hadn't really been around and then we found each other near the end.
He brought with him an eldest sister; who I thought I never had.
For the first time in my life ever, I felt a sense of belonging.
It wasn't until my wedding day; that I truly experienced this like never before.
My wedding had taken place a few years back; when I finally had realized, how much my father Frank really did love me.
It was my father Frank, who prompted Nick and the horse carriage to get there on time.
He was standing right there, where he is now and this is how I choose to remember him.
With all his flaws, there was a heart in him as pure as gold, but who really is perfect?
He never really judged anyone and how he made me smile at the end of a hard day; is how I wish to remember him and that he died a hero. Dad never gave up on me and I will never give up on him...

2nd Eulogy Sample (from his fiancé Megan)

Frank was wonderful and an incredible father; he loved his girls very, very much. More than anything he was a giving soul; a great friend to be around; always buying a round and giving everybody a good laugh...Frank has completely packed this place out and we will be having more of these to come in memory of his great wealth in friends and social affiliates he pledged a legion with...So I will keep this short for more is yet to come...

Sept. 26th, 2018

Public speaking for a pre-paid Funeral Service Ceremony:

The following is an introductory scenario sample: more details on the structuring to come (as this is a fairly simple observation from an actual scenario, that can be made for further study).
Interview with Purchaser/Beneficiary: Ask to look through their photo albums for example; then begin with the questions.
The following are just simple examples that were utilized in this scenario:

1) What were you like as a child ?
2) What did you want to be when you grew up?
3) List of mates from school?
4) First Job ?
5) First Marriage?
6) And all that to the heart of it; being her family stuff ?
7) Your first Christmas or your first loved one's experience with Christmas ?
8) Other memorable special events; like having the party of your life ?

Sept. 26th, 2018

Public speaking for a pre-paid Funeral Service Ceremony:(Continued)

Then the client starts to speak out by answering question #8: *Her husband John keeling over in pig muck at the farm.*

Client Speaks: " *Out of nowhere I had my gorgeous girl*"
"*This chronic illness of mine is like a piece of string and how long this piece of string is we simply do not know*" ?
Her doctor however said, she had a while to go just yet and that they cannot determine how long is this while.

As her client you have been given this information in the strictest of confidence and confidentiality; because only her husband knows and well she does not know when to come around if at all to telling anyone else about her dying…..

Now change the Officiant's role to be a niece/nephew and while in the same respect must keep the same level of confidentiality and then consider the "Rough Draft" starting to look as the following:

Writing The Eulogy of Aunt Faye:

Celebrant: How is uncle John taking it all ?
Aunt Faye: "*John likes to go out for long walks; all the way up to the log cabin*".
He was struggling with the whole idea already and now having to accept seeing his wife go off like this ?
For it all he blamed himself…

The Funeral Officiant & Ceremony

Preparing the Funeral Service Ceremony before a loved one dies: Talking about our Funeral Ceremony, can be difficult; on the other hand who will know our preferences as well as us, to plan it. By preparing exactly what music; readings and even the overall mood and theme of our own Funeral and Ceremony; it can take the stress and worry away from those we have leave behind.
A skeletal sample here shows, how the Celebrant can be real handy:

> Starting the Ceremony
> An Opening Reading
> Introduction
> Words to Soften Grief
> A daughter's Tribute
> Eulogy
> Readings & Tributes
> Committal
> Closing
> Benediction (non- religious)

Nearing the end and in Chapter V, a recap to expand on the above will be provided for the reader; so it can better start to make more sense.. After reading this book the competence of creating your very own Ceremony script and to ensure that a copy of it is kept safe somewhere when needed. As a Celebrant you will keep the many other scripts on file from whom shall ever come to you in need of such a service; this way a percentage of your fee will be required at the point of planning with the remainder being paid at the time of the Funeral.
It is all about authentic creative possibilities that we posses as Celebrants. "Public Speaking" is a skill. Establish a real connection so that the service you provide can generate you income.
Relate and communicate this skillful factor in; listen and understand, how to best articulate the narrative.

Back to the example of Writing The Eulogy For Aunt Faye:

Although the actual Ceremony at the day of service will be conducted by the local Vicar; You have been asked, by your Aunt to take down the following dictation:

Hello everyone and greetings.

We are gathered here today to celebrate the life and times of the legendary Faye Traynor.
She was very particular about this, so I mustn't fumble:

Request No. 1: No sobbing if you can help it.

Request No. 2: Happy stories not sad ones.

Request No. 3: Get real drunk but never by repeat the riding about in circles.

Writing The Eulogy For Aunt Faye:

Faye was a lot of things:

- A gifted mechanic.
- A farmer.
- Role model.
- Builder.
- Maker of the greatest casserole dish in town.
- She was also the best thing that ever happened to John Traynor.

Writing The Eulogy For Aunt Faye(continued):

Faye was a lot of things(continued):

- To the girl who turned up uninvited; she was an incredible mom to our Nora. Aunt Faye had given birth to her on Christmas Day of 1990 and had never felt love like this before. The hardest thing for Faye was in knowing that she would have to leave her only biological daughter in this way. Nora might have been her only real flesh and blood, but she did not stop there; she kind of ended up mothering us all.

It did not matter that she was only a Traynor by marriage; Faye was always there to turn to. She was there to greet us with a beverage and a cuddle; or a load of abuse, depending on what you did or did not do. She helped Wendy with Tracy; Lucy with Kane; repaired the things we thought that could never be fixed; because she was the glue now wasn't she?

Faye brought this mad family back together; time and time over again. Now she has taken it upon her; to face her greatest challenge with this illness and as she has with this Ceremony to plan the rest. I have never seen anyone show more courage; I think for those of us who really knew her, she was one heck of a woman.

May 23rd, 2019

(Excerpt to Sample) Public speaking for a pre-need Funeral Service Ceremony:

"On September 10th 2018 she was diagnosed for having Polycythemia vera and on May 23rd 2019 she had a heart attack. Resting peacefully in her living room, with her best dress on, when the Coroner pronounced her dead".

The final details can take place at the church; Funeral chapel; and/or home of the deceased, or family.
The following are given examples of what these sheets pertaining documents to be filled out by Clergy and or Religious Officials can look like and incorporated with their religious service; however not held as subject to, by this particular scenario; rather just blended in again with that of what Funeral Centres might already be providing and or other church affiliations:

Clergy Documents And Sample Sheets:

Name of Decedent: Faye Traynor   .

Date of Arrival to Canada:
_____.

Parents Name: Mother:_____.

                Father:_____.

Name of Spouse: _____.

Date of Marriage:_____.

The Funeral Officiant & Ceremony

Clergy Sample Sheets(Continued):

Name of Children(Spouse)/Grandchildren/Great Grandchildren

1. _____
2. _____
3. _____
4. _____
5. _____
6. _____

Siblings:_____ **Sisters** _____ **Brothers** _____ .

_____
_____
_____
_____
_____

Occupation:_____.

Accomplishmentrs:_____.

Clergy Notes continued:

Other Information:
_____

Location of Memorial Lunch:
_____

_____

Administrative files family profile of Clergy documents
Pre-need/paid   09/30/18   2:56 PM

In collaboration with, on the day of her passing and prior to the service the following information was imparted.
The Vicar made notes with the next of kin/purchaser; by asking her/him a few questions and just going over the final details(with them all involved).

Note: After and/or during Visitations at the Funeral chapel or any other place where the decedent is being kept for Vigil service(Wake). Following the next day Funeral and Burial/Cremation service(rite of Committal).
When one of its members dies, the church encourages the celebration of the Funeral Liturgy at a Mass.
Also - when a Mass cannot be celebrated, a Funeral Liturgy outside Mass can be celebrated at the church or in the Funeral establishment.

The Funeral Officiant & Ceremony

The Funeral Liturgy:

Is at the central most point of celebration to the Christian community for the deceased. The church can gather with family and friends of the decedent. To give praise for Christ's victory over sin and death, and bring the deceased closer with God's tender mercy of compassion; from the strength in the proclamation of the mystery called Resurrection. The Funeral Liturgy, therefore, is an act of worship, and not merely an expression of grief.
Given the example: A Mass might not be accepted for some and might not be practicing Catholics even when married into it; to suggest the preference of a more elaborate and inclusive as these services can be.
The following will again be adapted from the previous scenario to a regular and standard Pastoral service by a lady Minister.
Where Eulogies and other readings can be collaboratively accepted in this space of worship and throughout the Ceremonial entirety; including the officiating of a Celebrant; and or Funeral Director alike; as well as any other family member(s) appointed to and in this co-creative service to include as many as can be accommodated.

Given the Catholic example and that of most other Christian faiths alike from Orthodox to United: The same pretty much template Of these followed by a Graveside or cremation chapel(Committal service). From there all the other Ceremonies whether be it cremated remains scattering and/or other life celebrating tributes; they all fall under the category of a "Tribute" and/or "Memorial Service". Much more will be discussed and that of further detail. The following scenario will be given to conclude as one would with the middle part of service: From the standard Christian Bible-John 11:25 "Jesus said to her".

Continued from previous,
<u>(Excerpt to sample)Public speaking for a pre-need Funeral Service Ceremony</u>:

Faye Traynor ---------May 23rd 2019   Day of Service Saturday May 25th 2019

The Reverend: *"I am the resurrection and the life said the Lord. He that believeth in me and though he were dead; yet shall he live. Whom so ever liveth and believeth in me, shall never die".*

Welcome everyone to a service of celebration, for the life of our dear friend and neighbour Faye Traynor.
In our memories that they may be for ever lasting;
she was a blessed soul. Faye was surrounded by love in this life; she survived by her husband John; her pride and joy beloved daughter Nora and all her Traynor family.

In this moment perhaps the order for the Ceremony might differ in that of family request; and that we go no further deep before we can announce that Nora come up and say a few words before she changes her mind....

The Funeral Officiant & Ceremony

Continued from previous, (Excerpt to sample) Public speaking for a pre-need Funeral Service Ceremony:

Faye Traynor ---------May 23rd 2019   Day of Service   Saturday May 25th 2019

<u>Nora to the pulpit</u> : *"Stop the clocks and turn off the mobile Phones " Prevent the pigs from grunting and just let them roam" "She was my best friend and she was my mom; but today I feel all empty and alone. She said it how it was and she kept it real; with a heart of gold and nerves of steel. What you saw, you got ! When my dad married her, he hit the "Jack Pot". "Mom you meant more to me; than any words can say.*
I just wish I had tomorrow and not yesterday". "She might not have been my directional compass; but she was my mother. I have cherished her encouragement and I feel this strength forever within me still" "I loved you in life and forever will"!

<u>The Reverend</u>: Thank you Nora, that was so very touching. Forevermore this will echo and pass along from one heart to another. These are the sweetest words for Faye to hear and as whisperings into the doors of heaven. Faye also saw it to making certain she would be heard and have a say in this; through the voice of Lisa her words written down. Can we have her niece Lisa come up to the front please, you have been called.

Continued from previous,
(Excerpt to sample)Public speaking for a pre-need Funeral Service Ceremony:

Faye Traynor ---------May 23rd 2019   Day of Service Saturday May 25th 2019

Lisa Traynor: *"As difficult as the officiating might appear to be; my aunty wanted to Appoint me this position and to coordinate as best I could, this Ceremony".*
"We are here to celebrate the life and times of the legendary Faye Traynor. When aunt Faye asked me to do her Eulogy; I thought that she was drunk. I guess the next few minutes will determine, to whether this statement is true. She had a few requests about how this theme should go; I am worried she might come back to haunt me, should I not relay them all to you. What they are I really do not fancy that idea; because she scared me enough while she was alive".

Request No. 1: No sobbing if you can help it.

Request No. 2: Happy stories not sad ones.

Request No. 3: Get real drunk but never by repeat the riding about in circles.

"Before we get drunk, Faye had one more thing up her sleeve and I am certain you will be liking it". In her memory we welcome you all to the very first Pickering pig race, so if you please; she asked the theme be Funeral casual dress and no black". "One more thing..

That she requested everyone..... "**BE HAPPY !**"

Pre-need Vs. Pre-paid

The above was a "Pre-need" sample for a Ceremony service.
A pre-need is a Ceremony and/or Funeral arrangement and before it becomes an "At-Need"; it can be made amongst a family similar to a "Will" and that a Funeral home can hold on file.
Not subject to any binding contract however and without any financial investment, to suggest a contract be made.
A contract is a signed agreement between the parties and that do sign when coming into it; as such becoming a legal agreement.
Now a days without any financial backing, an agreement can be as the same as to interpret verbal; however never let it be this great deception of the two. Anything consented and in writing that has been signed; is as important as is the exchange of money for a service and/or product (to be taken seriously).
A Pre-paid is therefore just the same as a signed contract when money is involved. It must be so to take into consideration that it has now advanced from an interesting idea of giving your word to it, to an invested one of financial interest potentially accrued through time or not(depending on the contract). As a Celebrant and Ceremony Officiant; it is best to create the script and be paid for it up front. Make a copy for yourself; create a file and hang onto it; only when the client decides to contact you again, you can revise it with another price and depending on your services that you will be offering.

What is the relevance for a CONTRACT ?

The following 2 diagrams are samples of what the front and back of a legal size Contract might resemble:

ACIFC   CSOC

Funeral Ceremony Contract

BETWEEN   CONTRACT # _____

peerlessmoments.com
416 ___ ___ .
Toronto, Ontario
AND

PURCHASER NAME :   RECIPIENT NAME :

Name: _____   Name : _____

Address: _____   Address: _____

City, Province: _____   City, Province: _____

Telephone: _____   Date of Birth: _____

If applicable: Date of Death _____ AND Place of Death _____

Relationship to Recipient: _____ is the Purchaser of this contract between Peerless Moments
and with said owner Name: _____

Professional Services

Package (A) Standard
20 minute Ceremony to OFFICIATING/SPEAKING $ _____

5-8 minute Ceremonial Speaking
Package (B) Closing $ _____

10-15 minute Officiating/speaking Ceremony
Package (C) Budget $ _____

Package (D) 15-20 minutes
Graveside Ceremony $ _____

Package (E) from 40 minutes On.
Elaborate Ceremony $ _____

Package (F) To prepare a
Pre-Arranged Ceremony $ _____

Package (H) à la carte $ _____

Additional Services/Products

Mileage Charge $ _____ per/km _____ km _____ . $ _____

Other : _____ . $ _____

Other: _____ . $ _____

Other : _____ . $ _____

                                         Package Price $ _____
                                         Additional Services/Products $ _____
                                         Sub Total $ _____
                                         H.S.T. (at 13% & # presently N/A) $ _____
                                         TOTAL: $ _____
                                         Amount Paid (Deposit) $ _____
                                         Total Amount Owing: $ _____

The Funeral Officiant & Ceremony

Delivery time and location: The services and/or products contained in this contract will be delivered as outlined below. It is understood that some decisions may be made or changed subsequent to this contract. By signing this contract, the Purchaser consents to the delivery of the product(s) and/or service(s)

Event	Date	Time	Location	Confirmation

The Purchaser(s) agree(s) to pay the full amount owing within 5 days, after which interest will be calculated and charged in accordance with the terms of payment set out in this contract. Interest will be charged on any overdue amount at the rate of 4% per month (equivalent to 48% per annum) until the date payment is made in full.
Failure to Pay: The said 25% NON-REFUNDABLE DEPOSIT is to be made at the initial interview and the final agreed upon to be paid in full on completion of the Final Interview must be paid by the Purchaser.
In regards to the above provisions of the foregoing that can include other supplies and/or products as well in addition to the service and further more transcript/ceremony/package.
If the Purchaser(s) fails to make payment required under this contract to the Provider, all expenses of collection, including court/lien costs and all lawyer fees incurred by the Provider in pursuing the claim against the Purchaser(s) including any remaining fees if so to be affixed by the court(s) regarding any outcome of the judgment in such suit to be paid for by the Purchaser(s).
Third(3rd) Party Agreement: The Purchaser(s) acknowledges and agrees that the Celebrant Provider will be acting on behalf of, and only for as agent to the Purchaser(s); so to perform and/or officiate and oversee the Ceremony. As agent should require the need to fully engage with Funeral Home Directors and/or responsible staff representatives for the purpose of this Ceremony and/or clergy/religious officiates for the Recipient and on behalf of the Purchaser(s) this permission to be granted._____ To be given the permission to work along side and in collaboration; to be also granted_____ the accessed privileged information that normally might not be permitted under any such circumstance and/or privacy act. The Purchaser(s) are one in the same Purchaser(s) to the Funeral Service Contract given here to further agree for the Provider of this contract permission to form this alliance with respect in making sure with respect to be able to converse with each other freely any or all given information that is required for the co-operation and that which will benefit the client. In relevance to this third(3rd) part agreement should it also include other affiliates that it might include a joint effort for the purpose a semi-secular and/or religious officiate to partake with this Ceremony service are mentioned that Purchaser(s) also agree to give this permission so to work in full co-operation for the purpose of this said Ceremony.
Contract: This contract is binding on the Purchaser and the Provider and their respective heirs, successors and assigns, and will be governed by the law of the land. If another contract is made or is to be made in that given a conflict might arise in relation to this contract all proof must be verified with this other contract that the same Purchaser is consistent in both or all contract agreements pertaining to the Recipient must be verified and/or amended for this consideration. If there is more than one Purchaser; the obligations of the Purchaser(s) and this contract are joint and several.
_____ The Legal Authority as the Purchaser declares that he/she is to make, or charged with the responsibility for, in this or any other conjoining arrangements as the same Purchaser too in this contract.
Printing &Copyright Agreement: Many Funeral Ceremonies contain hymns, religious readings, poetry, excerpts, pop music-all of which the bereaved may wish to have printed in the order of Ceremony. Since a Funeral is a private function copyright holder's permission are not required; however should the text of any of the above require printing that a copyright exists in creative works such as the above for 70 years after the death of the writer(s) it is required the permission of the copyright holder(or their appointed agent) to be charged a fee. If it is only to be used for singing and/or exclusively for this said Funeral private function. That this order of service and/or client copy transcript not be duplicated and/or made other copies of. Within this said contract the _____ Purchaser(s) now made aware of and by so doing will take full responsibility of any breach to this affect unless copyrights are removed and/or said client/purchaser(s) full responsibility over any liabilities to the extent of being sued and/or takes this further copyright infringements there upon legally held responsible.
_____ **Business Price List**: The client/Purchaser(s) acknowledges having received copies of the business price list; and a consumer information Peerless Moments Brochure.

Peerless Moments is under the sole proprietorship and fully operated exclusively by Maria Arvanitidis.

_____   _____   _____
Ceremony Provider: Ceremony Purchaser   Date
                                                                    (print & sign name in full)

_____   _____   _____
Purchaser/Beneficiary   Funeral Services Purchaser   Date
(print & sign name in full)   (print & sign name in full)

__/ __/ __ **Contract**: The client(s)/Purchaser(s) acknowledges having received a copy of this contract.

What is the relevance for a CONTRACT ?

As great as it might be to have a contract and in the situation of such services alone; it is best to only take money in the immediate exchange of service and/or product.

A "Pre-Plan/pre-need" can make it possible to offer the service of a "Ceremony Draft" and that can later in the future be revised. An actual service pricing for a pre-need such as this; however the public speaking and officiating fee can be omitted. This way a file and contract can be created to come back to at a later date. The impact of a contract allows for a cooperative flow and with the complete spectrum to coordinate with the likes of others involved; that have also agreed upon and as said responsible, be made aware of this intention for the same outcome of purpose. With a contract the responsibilities do not get waivered by other power struggles and that might arise from miscommunication (when positions of authority become blurred) and any or all misconceptions thereof; upon other set agreements to the same however misleading outcome. The connection to cooperate in this way with all parties involved loosens the grip of any overpowers to control with from fears that might be perceived to be held as liable for. With a Ceremony contract the choice is made aware to clients that it is in their hands; and made by them to prefer the quality of selection. One day and hopefully after reading this book a better connection from the prior separation (over baring need to control) and other such power struggles will diminish. Now let us focus more on other aspects of a contract's value further. Again it must be noted, that a contract as great as it might be; it does not necessarily entail the need for a financial bind and/or investment. The following will be another given example: just the same as in your course study curriculum; however without the actual photos to include. Keep reading, more structured modules will be provided along the way; (step by step/templates) instructions and ideas.

The Funeral Officiant & Ceremony

What is the relevance for a CONTRACT?

For now let's take into consideration the following scenario and allow the imagination to explore a little the importance of all the many facets from the bigger picture. You are given the following information; however not necessarily in the right order.
Get used to having to take down information; taking information apart; as well as having to put it all back together. Perhaps some information might be missing, this is where the onus of having to call whom so ever you must have to and get in touch with, to obtain for any given situation. Additional correspondence can be made upon proper payment; to request for further learning and certification. In this case, timelines have been manipulated to fit in more than one scenario to sample and why it might have such relevance to forecast the importance of a pre/plan/need; as well as contract and as in the case before it.. Again it will depend upon the discretion to how it is preferred the many services and reflected from the creation of its packages and price list.

The significance of a Pre-Arrangement/ Pre-plan ?

What happens when a pet gets sick or loved one gets stricken with a chronic illness ? How can we come to terms with this thing known as anticipatory grief? How do we go bout it and to express the love that we are feeling for our loved in hospice care and/or on their way to passing over? The following was just that and had started from previous for a service held before for his older brother. The following could have been well served rather by a Pre-arranged Ceremony draft and now could have been further revised. Although these are two different events and based on the given information; can you see how much easier this Ceremony is to put together?

The significance of a Pre-Arrangement/ Pre-plan ?

You can imagine it so and restructure it from your pre existing Ceremony of Akba's brother ?
As a grey moving fog and moving past me now; was this my beloved cat "AKBA" ? He proved to Laura in December of 2019 that he definitely had a soul and that he survived death in a different dimension. Here he was in 2012 standing on her picnic table next to his brother who is in the Sun named Merlin.

(Where the photo would be) **PHOTO No. 1**

They were Flame-point Himalayans from the same litter. Then terribly five years later; In 2016 and as shown in the picture below: Merlin on the left became ill with cancer and the vet advised that she should have him put to sleep.

(Where the photo would be) **PHOTO No. 2**

For some reason Laura Bismuth could not bring herself to doing this. You can see in the photo Akba on the right hugging Merlin on the left. In this picture and during that time was when Merlin was becoming seriously sick.
Laura can recall during this time how Akba would help Merlin and hug him, as in the picture.

The Funeral Officiant & Ceremony

The significance of a Pre-Arrangement/ Pre-plan ?

Then one night, Merlin pushed his head into a corner of the room and Akba and Laura stayed close to him until one o'clock in the morning. Then out of no where and for no apparent reason; Merlin let out a "Yowl", so strong, it was as if you were coming back to life and protesting the force of death. Laura can remember how incredible his energy was that she was feeling after picking him up. In her mind she thought that; it was like he was saying "I'm not going to give up to this". She claims to this day how palpable this energy she felt from him was like, and then he went silent.
Laura and her brother buried Merlin the very next day on a hill next to her house.

It was then that she had called for help to put together and perform a Memorial Graveside service for him and to be held for Friday evening (just before Sun set).

Three years later by Christmas time in 2019 "Akba" was nearing eighteen years old. Suddenly Laura had noticed him becoming weak. He was having a hard time standing and walking. It was time again for Laura to be faced with this kind of decision about whether to take him to the vet; or try to hospice him.

(Where the photo would be) **PHOTO No. 3**

From that moment on Laura started carrying Akba everywhere. She would leave him downstairs at night so he could be next to a flat litter box and along with his water and food; that he barely ate. Wherever Laura placed Akba; he would purr, she loved him so much. Then one night he could not stand at all; is when Laura knew the time has come where she must take him to the vet.

The significance of a Pre-Arrangement/ Pre-plan ?

The next day she called her brother to ask him if he could meet her at the vet at noon. She cried with "Akba" and wrapped him in a towel for him to be warm; she then went to bed leaving him at the place that she had left him all the nights before.
At 4 a.m.; on her digital clock she woke straight up with adrenaline running; she heard a scratching at her bedroom door. Laura can remember jumping to the floor; she opened the door and there was "Akba". He had pulled himself up the entire stairs to her door; that he had not been able to do for months. Laura had then lifted him up and hugged him to her chest, in disbelief. How did he do this, she thought; when he could not stand up for even a few seconds.
A few hours earlier Laura sat back down in her bed against the pillow with Akba hugged inside her arms and against her chest. She just held him and he began to purr. They sat there together with him purring and with Laura holding him; unmoving for the next three hours. Laura knew she had to meet her brother, Bob at the vet at noon and she did not want to go; she wanted rather Akba to stay hugged in her arms forever.
On the next day Laura had arrived with Akba to the vet; while holding him they got the needle ready in the next room.
She wanted to continue holding him through that but then she could not bring herself to be able to. When her brother and the vet had asked her if she wanted to hold Akba during the shot; she suddenly could not stand the idea, of holding Akba when he would stop breathing. She thought she could get passed the emotion, but she started to cry again; even as she was describing this to you (as you were taking down these notes). While crying she had asked her brother (Bob) if he could instead hold Akba and when she put her face next to Akba's for the last hug; she thought he had the most beautiful blue eyes that she had ever seen and always so full of life.

The Funeral Officiant & Ceremony

The significance of a Pre-Arrangement/ Pre-plan ?

Then in two minutes Bob came back and put Akba in her arms again. Akba now was so still and the light in his open eyes was gone. The blue in his eyes was already changing to gold; an alien foreign gold, that symbolized to her of this beautiful soul's light leaving. She could recall hearing herself calling out in the vet lab room; "Akba, where did you go?" "what part of you has left?" "I don't want you to leave." Then she really broke out in tears after that she could remember doing so; as her brother took Akba and her back home. Finally around midnight she sat there hugging her arms around her knees; just as she had been hugging Akba a few hours earlier in the morning and after his miraculous climb up the stairs for the last time.

They are to bury Akba in a beautiful small casket; that her brother Bob made, to put him next to his brother Merlin and on the same hill. The rest of the day she was literally sick in heart and stomach trying to communicate with you. Sometimes things might not make any sense and on these various levels of sensitivity, you must try to use discernment. As you also must be aware of the level of vulnerability; as well as when making notes, the confidentiality of such a relationship, between your clients. For this reason, it is always best(before hand) to "ask if you can record the conversation" and while paying closer attention to them when they speak(will allow for better focus on your clients). Take brief moments to make written notes; because it might distract from the focus on their attention to go deeper and maybe even a little off the mark(is good for spicing up indirectly and creatively the Ceremony further).

Notice that in fact some of this was taken from a pre recorded interview; so to experience first hand, what you will be facing.

The significance of a Pre-Arrangement/ Pre-plan ?

Then just like that morning when Akba was outside the door; it was 3 a.m. on the digital clock. The door flew open as she had described it. In the dark of her bedroom, she found herself on her back and in a Cat Yoga pose; as she could recall, when she used to do years and years of Yoga. Laura finds that she sleeps on her side mostly; however this time she found herself on her stomach and stretched out in a Cat Pose. Never in her life before this night had she ever found waking herself this way. She found herself looking straight above her bed board and looking right into what appeared to be, this oval.

The image was a yellow, bluish, white light; all the way around. The oval, stretched out at about 2-3 feet in diameter and inside of it, seemed like energy was pulsing out this blue white and yellow light exhibit. To her amazement and at her lucid waking state; there right in the middle of this oval and with this energy was Akba: blue eyes; fluffy white hair; standing absolutely strong and alive. Laura jumped to reach out and grab him; is how she could recall waking up to find herself in such a way. This portal was so vivid and as she was trying to grab for Akba; she saw a grey path like spiral; it was doing a curve and it was going into something that looked like a tunnel. Laura swore she was not exaggerating; because it was where her cat Akba was and as if he were sitting in the front of one of these Einstein-rosen bridges between timelines. She saw Akba as she could recall to be sitting there with something behind him in a spiral; it was just as clear as day to her. Even though she had been grabbing air and she was hoping it would be Akba; she remembered crying out "you came back" "you came back, where are you now?" "Please show me, where are you now?" This is one of the internal soul questions and goals that we all might be having to try to come to terms with. In living life, where does our soul at the moment of what we call death.

The Funeral Officiant & Ceremony

The significance of a Pre-Arrangement/ Pre-plan ?

Should the soul have any eternal recycling in many, many body containers after resurrection ? This might be one of the most important issues for all of us to come and reconcile with in our own time during this process of grief and to take some kind of confidence and reassurance. The faith that in life we must prepare for the inevitable life there after and this is what Akba taught Laura. Akba coming back the night of his mortal body death to show Laura that he was still alive in another dimension; was one of the most important moments in her life. Since then Laura has come to realize that the most important thing for her was the soul part of us on earth.

Note: The more you get to know, the better outcome for the Ceremony and for future ones to come.

Laura believes it as a force and like a field that she described it; an archive of lives that recycles way into infinity and back.
Like photons of light to travel at 186,000 miles a second where mass is infinite and time stops; The photons of light and perhaps souls experience all of time as a single moment. Where past, present and future are one; Albert Einstein's recollection as a fact it was this oneness of awareness. Some say that the soul is infinite and that it possibly can go on forever. About the soul and dying we can all be in awe of such a mystery that day by day unfolds for us this way and in the passing of this life into the here and after that it might be venturous to say it goes on to infinity, forever and ever lasting just like the universe.

The significance of a Pre-Arrangement/ Pre-plan ?

Like Laura we can lay in bed at night to contemplate this over in our minds; to deeply dare to dream like she had with her beloved Akba and his crossing over to the other side.
This consciousness that would be all knowing simultaneously aware of it's infinite universe and floating state as a mist or hazy blob like substance to a destination of its own authentic individuation once more to be enlightened of its presence within a body made physical.
In this instance the space was open for some counseling and just by listening to a very intelligent conversation.
The treatment to clear some trauma, it can be a very healthy sign to witnessed and when others in this case express their grief in such a way. The Pastoral services were rendered in this case by a Metaphysical Spiritual Minister and performed likewise; not that different from a Funeral Celebrant Ceremony service. As it stands it is not very likely to have a 3 hour Baptist collaboration service for a pet. Although quite a number of independent Funeral Homes have accepted a more ecological view point; it only goes as far as to include a limited spectrum factor of conditions and that would be imposed upon(commission based) a call list, of "<u>affordable</u>" Celebrants. In most cases although not legalized in certain cities; Funeral services for pets can involve a burial service in a cemetery. Some Funeral Centres do provide the space for a Memorial Tribute; after the common cremation can take place and with the selling of such products as urns; however not very likely to obtain a Reverend of this nature. This especially is where a Ceremony from a Celebrant can be made most useful.
Stay tuned and let us continue expanding these services, through out this book.

The Funeral Officiant & Ceremony

Metaphysical (Spiritual) Ministries, Pastoral and Funeral Ceremony Services:

The Metaphysical Spiritual parishes are legalized entities and like any other religious ministry it is; however not limited to interfaith complexities. Nor is the Ceremony that it officiates in this way subject to be under the Christian and/or any other hierarchy collaboration. Adhering to all the laws of nature, it can organize as well as alchemize all energetic equations; into something that will benefit its focus of intention on and in service to the greater good. As a "Bespoke" religious fit for any given occasion; and this does especially include the Funeral/Memorial process.

The Celebrant does and can have many peers, it can look up to for the purpose of pastoral collaborative, co-creation and this most definitely can include such a ministry. Most of the time it may come off of as absurd for a Pope and/or Arch-Bishop or even Bishop and its Monarchy; this does include for all denominations of Priesthood/Pastoral Brotherhood alike. To victimize here is not the answer; nor that one to its own alliance of awareness, is better than another(competitive recognition of their Sovereign given Light)anything less than what they serve as Master.

Rather a Celebrant is released from all such conditional programs; to reflect from its creative pallet. We might not pledge a legion to the sinister and more serious of the above Abrahamic, authoritative sculpting and from the same clay perhaps do not originate.

A Metaphysical Minister brakes through the clay to go deeper where the gold can be seen. In this way the Celebrant (from a Heart Centered space) might in fact be made from the same cloth; and have a lot of similarities to consider. Applying mental transmutation, unlimited thereby and coming directly from the "Heart to Soul" connection. In honouring every faith, because "Faith" is "Metaphysical".

Metaphysical (Spiritual) Ministries, Pastoral and Funeral Ceremony Services:

Freedom is the key to "Soul" and the ability to express in a more subtle spiritual way; this is at the source of its enlightenment and motive to inspire the pristine aspects from all religious conglomerations. "Faith" does not require a religion; however religion does require a certain level of "Faith". At the apex of such a non traditional approach and that a Non-Secular/Secular can find resonance to.

The Celebrant by no means are they a HAT(Non-Secular Toronto community) "Humanist" and have no obligations as of yet by legal bind to licence. A Celebrant can offer their services anywhere (even off Planet) with no conditional limits and can be civil, as well as faith transparent. This is where they stand out and differ from the rest of the pack. Non-traditional in that "Faith" forms religion and not the other way around; in this way we can go deeper to find our client's personal philosophy from which to <u>Bespoke a Ceremony</u>.

Canadian Society Of Celebrants, is thereby an organization that can better be identified to group and promote such dedicated souls; be they Agnostic and even Humanistic-Atheist, all paths are welcomed. Although Celebrants might walk the same path of spiritual philosophy as their religious counter parts that would include a Metaphysical Spiritual parish; by no means is the Canadian Society Of Celebrants in any kind of legal and Religious Ministry affiliating bind.

<u>Metaphysical(Spiritual) Ministry's Mission</u>: serenity, inner peace, sacred synergy and wholeness; that is in alignment with the harmony; of all that is divine light resonance and authentic individuations, expressed from this celestial being of oneness. The alignment of organic pulse/rhythm from our heart beat to that of nature's and the entire universal well being, for all existence.

The Funeral Officiant & Ceremony

Non-Denominational Vs. Multifaith:

As mentioned in the previous; a Celebrant can be "Non-Denominational and Multifaith". What does this even mean? The great schism began dividing the Christian church into Orthodox(Eastern) all the way to the far left church of Rome in the Western. From the 16th century reformation begot Lutheran-→ Protestant→Anglican → Quakers(Religious Society).
From the Anglican Church The world Council of Churches went off to form United sects of all sorts and as they changed observers from the left to right→ Roman Catholic Vatican Council → Babtist→ Presbyterian→ Methodist→Salvation Army. From there other sects begot included: Church of Jesus Christ and that of Latter-Day Saints; Seventh-Day Adventist→Church of Christ and King→Christian Science→Disciples of Christ→ Just from the Protestant alone over 300 other denominations; including the Christadelphians. From the Apostles Creed of the Roman Catholic left to the Russian/Greek/Syrian/Armenian/Coptic(Egyptian/Ethiopian). This is just a sample of the far and few in between of denominations (The Evangelical Lutheran/Jehovah's Witnesses/Mennonite)that Christianity alone to the far side of Judeo Christian Zionism. As we start approaching those other faiths that are non-Christian we again can come into different variations of the same but not the same that split off into denominations. Non-denominational can be interpreted to mean not of one religion practiced; it can give it the right of way for a non religious official and rather a Celebrant Officiant.
Non-denominational however is limited to Abrahamic teachings and that some Celebrating Life Ministries do claim themselves as Celebrants to master over. Not all legally authorized are allowed to represent themselves as "Non-Denominational"; but can in fact be represented as "Multifaith", such as and in the case of the Metaphysical(Spiritual) Ministries(are indeed ordained).

Non-Denominational Vs. Multifaith :

As we keep on going on and might have missed a few (Pentecostal to Polish Catholic); Hare → Krishna→Hinduism Islam-→Jainism→Judaism→Native Aboriginal and CreeNations→Rastafari→Sikhism-→Wiccan -
→Taoism→Buddhism and Zoroastrianism. Deism/Atheism as well as Humanism will be further explored under their very own title and to expand their meaning. The provision of spiritual and religious care in Ontario is supported by the member faith traditions which comprise the Ontario Multifaith Council on Spiritual and Religious Care; they have helped throughout the years to re-define the role of a Chaplain. Creatively reinventing the religious bodies to accept the growing population at a national level is this Goal. What the main focus must be on the spirit and its intent; the Celebrant must qualify and to respectfully reflect. Indeed, a heavy study it can be, the Funeral Ceremony and Celebrant path; not one that can be obtained within a few days of training. Do not feel misguided by this statement; there is nothing wrong in being charitable and picking up more training from other places.

A level of discernment on just how much you're willing to invest and where, is entirely up to you. Simply go at it with no comparison of any time restraints. This book wants for the reader and at their own pace to gain an independent footing and platform before it; rather it will empower and not force your disempowerment of choice with the likes of every other association to co-dependently join in.

Canadian Society Of Celebrants wants to empower every person who picks up this book and to read into its mastery with interest. Whether you choose to further qualify yourself into an alliance with and as an independent entrepreneur; to carryon the torch of training others, is entirely up to you, the reader.

This is the ultimate way of joining forces ! Is it not?

The Funeral Officiant & Ceremony

What are the Celebrant's Responsibilities?

A Funeral Celebrant, or thereby a student of such a role must own it with great confidence. Your responsibility is to engage with the client/family that has reached out and to establish the connection. Make contact with the family and methodically record details of the decedent's life, so that what is written depicts their true character. Collaborate with the bereaved family and/or friends, to co-create a portrait together and the outline of the. It is from this kind of sensitivity that will build your confidence to properly prepare and deliver a "Bespoke Ceremony". Care enough to help and support family and other mourners who are coming to terms with their loved one's death; because that is the motive for this plan.

Atheist/Humanist and Civil Celebrants:

The starting point for all Celebrant Funerals is Secular, i.e. non-religious. The more important principle is that the words said express, record for posterity, and honour the life of the person who has died. Our Ceremony tells the life story, marks the achievements, and praises the ideals and ambitions of the life of the individual we have lost. Most Celebrant Ceremonies are Secular and non-religious; they have been known to have client making requests for them to include times of silence, the Lord's Prayer, the 23rd Psalm and, as the family of the person who has died specifically requests it to add the following: For the purpose of putting together a more meaningful non-denominational Christian service and/or a Semi-Secular Ceremony; more will be expanded upon and in further detail later on.

Atheist/Humanist and Civil Celebrants:

Other Scriptures can include: (Psalm 46:1-2; 46:10-11;Psalm 34:18Psalm103:8-17Ecclesiastes 3:1-8) (Isaiah 41:10,13; John 10:27-29;11:1-4"Prayer of Jesus"; John 11.17-27; John 14.1-6; Mathew 5:1-16Romans 8:37-38 and 15:13; Job 1:211;Luke 2:29-32&12:27; Corinthians 15:42-57 as well as 2 3:1-5 and 4:16-15:8; Philippians 1:20-23 as well as 4:7,19,20; 1 Thessalonians 4:13,14&18;Hebrews 6:18-19 and Revelation 21.1-7). Canadian Society Of Celebrants are not subject only to Judeo-Christian and most importantly, not limited to Abrahamic structures of belief systems.

Civil means just that the person performing the Ceremony does not require to be registered by any official licensing body.
A Civil Celebrant is not that common; because more training to certify or at the very least educate the public and (like this book might) to help empower the confidence that it will take, for an unordained layperson to perform such a tasks.
Although Agnostic was not mentioned here to take into consideration and from the many other non Abrahamic philosophies: Canadian Society Of Celebrants honours all individual beliefs and idealisms of spiritual expression; including Agnostic/Humanist and Atheist (to be recognized and valued for their painful and emotional needs as well).
In order to have the ability we must learn their ways of preference and from here everything can better be more simplified. Agnostics tend to lean toward the unknown and make it known. Agnostic has got to be one of the oldest religions into faith and the unknowable truths. It can bring much depth to any Ceremony and script; by bringing certainty into the unknown mysteries and able to grasp them into meaningful experiences. Atheist are quite similar to Humanist in their services. Both offering appropriate Memorials to those who lived their lives without religious affiliation and reject the typically religious views associated with life and death.

The Funeral Officiant & Ceremony

Atheist/Humanist and Civil Celebrants:

At these Atheist services there is no specific reference to an afterlife, as Atheists do not believe in any deity. Instead, the Funeral services are a Tribute to the life the deceased lived. Loved ones that are left behind are acknowledged, and the deceased's life is remembered through memories. At an Atheist Funeral, it is best to avoid platitudes like "she's in a better place now" or "he's watching us from heaven now." While these kind of comments are usually taken as intended expressions of comfort and sympathy; they can just as easily be avoided. In most cases religious attendees would not feel out of place or offended by a Humanist Ceremony.
The focus of the event will center on sincerity and affection for the deceased and his or her family and close friends.
At most Humanist services, family, friends and even acquaintances may be asked to share their fond memories with others in attendance. Atheist cremation or burial are common Funeral practices. Whether or not there is an open casket is largely dependent upon individual preferences and circumstances.
If the deceased's wishes were not made known prior to the Funeral, the family will make such a decision. An Atheist service can be held at any time. Some choose to hold services before burial, some at Graveside, and still others opt for a Memorial service sometime after the burial or cremation. Music, religious readings and hymns are not part of an Atheist Funeral service. Songs and readings are still used, however. Favourite songs and poems or other readings may be shared during services. Classical music as well as modern favourites may be selected. Sometimes, a person has a chance to make decisions regarding the Funeral before death. In these cases a person may select arrangements according to his or her wants and desires.

Atheist/Humanist and Civil Celebrants:

Atheist services bring a sense of closure to family members and close friends, and are an important part of the grieving process. The atheist Funeral service gives loved ones a chance to express their sorrow and pain at such a devastating time. At this time of loss it is appropriate to show support to the family through Memorial charitable donations, memorial flowers, and meal preparation.

A Tradition Funeral order of service may include the following:
Musical Prelude
Introduction / Words of Welcome
Prayers
Scripture Readings
Musical Selections/Hymns
Formal Reading of Obituary
Eulogy/Life Tribute
Brief Informal Tributes
Thank you and Acknowledgements
Viewing of Deceased
Closing/Benediction

Non-Traditional Order of service (Funeral and Memorials)
Introduction / Words of Welcome
Opening Music
Readings
Musical Selections
Formal Readings
Moments of Silence/Meditation
Eulogy/Life Tribute
Brief Informal Tributes
Thank you and Acknowledgements
Viewing of Deceased
Closing

Atheist/Humanist and Civil Celebrants:

Humanist Funerals, or Memorials, allow friends, relatives and acquaintances to express their feelings and to share their memories with warmth, love and sincerity. Humanist Funerals/Memorials also recognize that not everyone wants a sorrowful Ceremony; but instead a Ceremony that celebrates the life and accomplishments of the person. They try to meet with or speak to the family or friends who are most closely connected with the person who has died and learn as much about the person as possible, so that the Funeral or Memorial Tribute "justly captures" the life and personality of that person. They welcome your ideas for readings, music and, if required, make suggestions suitable for the kind of Ceremony you want; some are even open to making themselves available for pet Funerals. A recent increasingly popular and preferred alternative to a Humanist service is a Civil service. This is also a non-religious Ceremony and completely neutral in its delivery.

The difference here between them is that a Humanist Officiant, though whilst providing a valid and meaningful non-religious Funeral Ceremony must endorse their Humanism differences in certain phrases that are used as part of the Ceremony.

For most people this is not a problem. It's hardly noticeable(until addressed) because it blends in with the Humanist theme of the Ceremony. These type of Ceremonies are not very flexible in their approach when it comes to religious content during the Ceremony. For instance if some members of your family or perhaps some of the congregation have a strong religious faith and it is your thought that the deceased may have wished to have acknowledged that faith by the saying of a prayer or the reading of a short extract from the bible, then that would not normally be allowed. Instead you would be offered the opportunity to do it silently and privately during the quiet time of Remembrance.

Atheist/Humanist and Civil Celebrants:

Most people are happy to go along with this arrangement even though it's not quite what they would have liked.
Once again let us be clear on what the due diligence in performing a Civil Ceremony for the Common Funeral Celebrant is: Civil just means that anyone with some know how and with no licence requirement or regulatory body to be acknowledged by; can perform these services.
To take the place of the Minister or Priest at the Funeral. They are dedicated to composing and conducting a Ceremony focused on the life of the deceased. A good Civil Funeral Celebrant will create a "Bespoke Ceremony" for the individual that truly reflects from the decedent's life. They will work closely with the family to ensure that the Ceremony is envisaged in the way that will support them in their grieving process and preparing for the Funeral.

What can be included in this fee?

A personalized service from the point of booking.
At least one meeting to gather information about the deceased and Funeral Ceremony, if necessary other meetings can be arranged. Advice and suggestions in regards to music, readings, timings etc. if required. At least one draft of the Ceremony sent to you to ensure it is what you envisaged.
Re drafts if necessary until you are happy with the words and format. Consultations with your Funeral Director to try and meet all your needs. A "Bespoke Ceremony", centred on the life of the decedent. A presentation copy of the Ceremony.
Canadian Society Of Celebrants are professionals who work with families to design a service that is customized to their cultural, religious, and spiritual needs. They are trained to help arrange both "Secular and Non-Secular" Celebrations.

The Funeral Officiant & Ceremony

Atheist/Humanist and Civil Celebrants:

Celebrant services are not limited to Celebrations of Life. They often work with people planning a Traditional Funeral or Memorial services as well. Many Celebrants are qualified to take on the role of Officiant as well as helping to plan the service. There are a few Ministers (usually retired) who are more than happy to perform a more low key religious service.
This means focusing less on the religious aspect of the service and more on the eulogy and tribute to the deceased. Often many religious references are dropped in favour of poetry and prose. Perhaps this type of Ceremony might appeal to you, then your Funeral Director will know of a local accommodating Minister. Civil Ceremonies are an excellent way of obtaining a personalized non-religious or semi-religious Funeral Ceremony and is an option well worth exploring. Unfortunately though not all areas have Civil Celebrants. However, ask your Funeral Director because if that is the case it may be possible to get a Civil Celebrant from a different area to come in for you. So now these days when arranging a Funeral you will be specifically asked by the arranger if you would prefer a Church Minister, a Humanist Officiant, or a Civil Celebrant. In other words do you want a religious service, a non-religious Humanist or non-religious, semi-religious Civil Ceremony. All three have there own rightful place and role to play in their services for the dead and the bereaved, they are by no means the only choices but they are the most popular. Of course one of the other options available to you is to take on the responsible and honourable role of Celebrant yourself. If the deceased was a family member or personal friend; then what better tribute could you afford them than to officiate at their Funeral Ceremony? Why not provide the appreciative mourners with the ultimate personal touch?

Atheist/Humanist and Civil Celebrants:

Each person or family's circumstances are different and individual to themselves it would be impossible to provide an all purpose reference to suit every occasion. Throughout this book will be provided several different example scenarios and scripts to work from. These can be tailored to suit your own particular situation and the needs of the people involved.

The information provided here is designed to help show you how to officiate a Funeral Ceremony. After the Funeral has been arranged through a Funeral Director and that the Ceremony will be either non religious or semi religious in content. This will impart with you and the many other participants who will read on just how to be able to Officiate and/or play a part in the proceedings. This will ensure that you all can work in harmony as smoothly as possible on the day. Logistics, timing and co-ordination are so important and you will only have the one chance to get it right.

The Final Draft:

Exactly just as mentioned before and from the book to find we must make room for improvements always.
Whether it be revised later 5 years up the road or the few day and/or day before the actual even is to take place:
Always go over everything when the day come for revising. Whether it be online communication to go over the details and confirm from the person who you are actually receiving the money for this service.. For the final draft gather around if you have to as you did before and confer over everything that has been incorporated well. This is the time for any extra little details that the families had and to why an added value for a pre-paid draft occurs to benefit for all. John Traynor was going through some old photos(that he had brought forward);the following reminded him of something that he would like to share with us as he reminisced:

The Funeral Officiant & Ceremony

The Final Draft:

(Where the photo would be) **PHOTO No. 1**

You have been asked to make adjustments to your draft from the following information and to incorporate perhaps the following as a consideration...What will you do?

Cont. putting together John's Eulogy:

(Where the photo would be) **PHOTO No. 2**

Faye and John belonged to a band and is how they first met in this pub from the photos given. He can recall the "Guild Pack" and from these photos he had rummaged; a reunion taking place down at her old favourite pub. This one night was her final gig with the "Guild Pack 2.0". John can remember that Saturday evening very well and mentioning to her about the line up as they had known it. The only thing that had changed was the line up to get in and depending on how you looked at it; some things might have changed but they have improved. Some things did however appear to stay the same; it was at that moment looking into her eyes remarking just how beautiful she was to him that night. Only but to say "Some things always dare to stay the same".

The Final Draft: (cont.)

You have been asked to make adjustments to your draft from the following information and to incorporate perhaps the following as a consideration…What will you do?

Cont. putting together John's Eulogy:

(Where the photo would be) PHOTO No. 3

In this photo after the band "2.0 Guild Pack" playing "up on a mountain top" lyrics and an up beat song as their country single called "HILL BILLIES ROCK & ROLL NIGHT" !

Faye Traynor had a passion for playing the violin and got all dressed up for the occasion as did her Hubby John.

This was the night that they had renewed their vows to one another. This would never be, nor should it be missed from any Ceremony; to give thanks in knowing the only true love of his life and soul mate (all dressed up in her wedding gown).

Chapter II

Resistance/Trauma/Shock:

As mentioned from before in chapter one, from the denying to believe a death has occurred. The trauma is most evident when dealing with palliative and chronic deaths; as was the experience with Laura and her cats. A prolonged inevitable death is as and can be as shocking as the resistance to deny an acute incident that has taken a young life. Every person has their own capacity of tolerance and readiness to accept the needless waste of life. These types of Ceremony tend to be much longer and more somberly pronounced. The meaning of a Celebrant can have a resentful connotation when dealing with young deaths; however less it might be though to call it the Celebration of a life as it might with someone who had the chance to fully live it. Compassion and mindfulness must play a key role for this kind of discernment must be well served when dealing with a family with a sudden loss.

As one might be experiencing the trauma of resisting to let go of someone dying; the other might be feeling shock from a sudden impact. These numbing sensations can very well be experiences that everyone must succumb to eventually; perhaps not necessarily in any order in particular and that we must work through, in our own time. By learning from our own personal experiences, we then can better hold an open space for others in this way, as best we can.

Different Types of Funeral Tributes:

Can be presented by almost anyone; anywhere and with or without the decedent present. Tributes can be Themed: Re-model the environment, as well as the music, into a theme loved by the deceased. More will be explored with Military/Police and Fire Fighter's protocol. A eulogy can also be written into a tribute which praises the deceased and is usually presented by the CELEBRANT and/or an immediate family member(s), a close friend(s) or Clergy.

Eulogy/Tribute/building of a Portrait & Misconceptions.

Sometimes participants might want to take longer than their given 5to10 minute slot for a eulogy; it can mislead the public view (when the Ceremony is not A "Tribute"). Ceremony by another name as to pay "Tribute" and in what they are about to say to separate them apart from just a eulogy; rather take longer as to create a separate segment from within the Ceremony as a theme(similar as Semi-Secular event). An example will be given in the next chapter, with the "Anatomy of the Ceremony".

The Ceremony script is all about building the portrait of the person and/or the loss of a pet. The eulogy is at the heart of this portrait; however a partial narrative and not so much the historical biography description, nor is it a "Tribute".

The Tribute on the other hand is just another name that would describe the type of Ceremony; in the same way as a "Celebration Of Life". Tributes/Memorials they are names given to describe the theme and type of service.

Eulogies are only partial aspects of the Ceremony script; hopefully after going through this handbook, it can be made more clear these misconception. The sharing of stories and giving praise are these allotted moments that collaboratively go to make a Ceremony script. Sometimes it might not even be included in the script and must be well adjusted to make room for it by giving it a time slot. A Tribute is an expanded condolence more or less; that can be made to blend within a eulogy and not by any means necessarily the entirety of the Ceremony. A Tribute of Remembrance, rather than a sad occasion of having to say "goodbye"; why not incorporate a Funeral Remembrance Ceremony for the deceased.

These joyful memories can be made great Tributes of comfort and support to surviving friends and family members while grieving. It is best to select a Tribute which you are comfortable with and which speaks to your loved one's memory.

The Funeral Officiant & Ceremony

The Eulogy & Ceremony Script:

It is always in good practice to be prepared with a full-on eulogy; even when the mourner is the main speaker. Along with all the other participating speakers, the Officiant is you and therefore your responsibility; in case that anyone should falter and for the Ceremony to be on cue. Always make certain that you have copies of all the participating speakers; it not only makes for a great Keepsake Ceremony Script. Otherwise the script will have holes of incompletion; that can reflect poorly on the overall performance and memory from the event. With this kind of experience you will be able to start and finish on cue. The bereaved rarely have any idea of what a "brief Ceremony" is and the onus is left up to the Celebrant to set clear markers, as well as figure out the venue's conditional time restraints. After the Introduction, it is customary to lighten the service with some words of comfort and to honour the memory of the deceased. There are many verses and poems that can be used; as a Celebrant you also have the choice of recreating from your own. This can also motivate all other participants to "be not scared of authenticity". Readings, Eulogies & Tributes: The heart of the Ceremony; Introducing the Eulogies and other speakers. The eulogy is the key to the entire Funeral Ceremony's narrative. This personal tribute can be split from those with an intimate knowledge of the deceased; the children wanting to contribute and can be of a great asset to share their thoughts with. The Celebrant must make a list of all the names of other contributors in order to facilitate an introduction for them. When they write their tribute down ask them to provide a copy; in case you need to step in for them if the situation demands. Prepare and check your eulogies of the person's life on record within your script. It is through a meaningful script that the Celebrant qualifications are to write and deliver.

The Eulogy & Ceremony Script:

The eulogy is distinct from reminiscences, and is central to a proper Ceremony. Not always do we have any form of relationship with the decedent and it is rare to speculate that we may already know quite a bit about them. In order to deliver a befitting true to memory and sincere eulogy speech/tribute and Ceremony get as much information on this person as possible. The First call and initial interview will be further looked after this and just how exactly to go about the correct questions to ask and also the "Interview Check List". Remember that this speech is not about you; it is about the deceased. Sometimes speakers make the mistake of talking more about themselves than the person everyone is here to honor and celebrate.

The best eulogies often are those that focus on your personal thoughts and memories of the deceased. Although the eulogy can become a tribute to commemorate, with praise and honour; remember the total allotment of time restrictions.

Within the Ceremony the value of its contributors might be to discuss the decedent's early family years; while another is mentioned by the Celebrants who speaks about the decedent's career on behalf of that business affiliate. Another person might help in the description and as a friend to speak about the decedent's character. As for the eulogy it is best to share the many stories of life lessons and experiences that have changed us and through the various involvements with the deceased(grandchild might address the love).

With a more elaborate Ceremony, will pay proper tribute to the deceased person; it rarely takes less than 45 minutes and can go up to and/or well over an hour. The process begins with the initial consultation, preparation, correction and another confirmation and/or rehearsal consultation. The onus is on the Celebrant to officiate the order of the ceremony. Gather as many memories and write out your brainstorm within the structured guide and/or template.

The Funeral Officiant & Ceremony

The Eulogy & Ceremony Script:

Add some quotes to describe a person's character and create the interest with some adjectives, to capture their essence with; this will greatly reduce the speech and give it impact. Other options are to include a favourite poem of the deceased, or a prayer.

The Ceremony is a portrait and it is comprised of one eulogy or many. During the initial interview, a family gathering is imperative to hold a meeting; whereby the support and significance is founded in the recounting memories of as many stories:

Where and where they were born; education; marriage/children; brothers/sisters; special accomplishments and achievements; life events; special beliefs; what they left behind as a legacy and other such memories will be further discussed. Also making some acknowledgement of those who passed before and that had close significance to the deceased. Maybe the family might want to take the time to gather this information from each member when they come around before hand; and/or hold a private gathering to save the many hours with the Celebrant. As more and more relate their stories; to reminisce this way and into the healing process of their grief, begins. Not every fact and detail will be imparted; however it is always best to have more variety than less. Creatively we must bring about the central eulogy; the reminiscences, poetry /quotations/ symbolic excerpts, and musical choreography. Contacting the Funeral Celebrant first, before contacting a funeral director has always been the way; however not everyone can be made visible this way. Rather than the Funeral Celebrant making recommendations; why not get all teams on board to work cooperatively in a union of great collaboration. There are some excellent Funeral Directors but many are unsympathetic to the quality of the "Ceremony"; they naturally prefer to emphasize on the non-ceremonial elements.

Why not change that rumour as of now !

YOU GET WHAT YOU PAY FOR

From the time it takes to inform the grieving families and friends to come around and help arrange the Ceremony(to revise and then refine the script); it will take at minimum, anywhere from 3-5 working days, to prepare a quality script. The writing of the Ceremony, the preparation of the eulogy, and the preparation and checking of all elements typically takes between 10 and 30 hours. What will be your minimum payment requirement? Start from that minimum requirement and work up, the less work we do the better for the family to get involved and gather what they wish for us to put together. Otherwise we can get into a school of thought where no one will be able to afford us. Some Funeral homes will filter through and select the most affordable candidates to represent their firm. Celebrants have been known to make between $50 to $100 per hour, depending on qualifications and experience. Let's face reality for a moment and where we must start off from. All across the board and given the location, it must be similar to what the Clergy charge and on the service they provide; is how we get our answers to adapt with.

Hence the reason for the made few select role model Celebrants and poster boys and girls. To the traditional way of thinking, and that best reflects for such a service to take place; a Memorial Tribute is more than just a message. It is the watered down culturally religious act; that otherwise and alternatively best can represent in its image, to provide the Ceremony. The Funeral home might suggest, it is "LGBTQ" friendly; unfortunately there is a lack for what is real amongst the uniformity for tribe. The confusion to discard for any authenticity and from a place of (held in judgments) weakness; to whom at surface level might just be, the traditional candidate for this role.

At the end of the day "It is business as usual" !

The Funeral Officiant & Ceremony

YOU GET WHAT YOU PAY FOR

Wouldn't it be nice, to get over such old world concepts of doing business ?

Looking at the nuts and bolts of it, our worth might be valued by "<u>Performance Base</u>" and not so much on a "<u>Need Base</u>".

As unfortunate death might be to consider, the need makes it a profitable and fortunate business. Do not be fooled by the corporate Funeral establishments, when they refuse to see your worth. Sometimes the need and drive requires competition to create a wobble effect; that otherwise the stalemate of a win/win and stable situation might bring in the long term loss for everyone. By lowering our self worth, we lose respect from others and likewise the same outcome begets as it would, by standing firm to honour our worth. How many hours do we actually spend on the Ceremony script alone? For example: consider not only the final product and there is your answer; on how much a Ceremony script alone must cost. Hopefully this handbook will truly connect all parties of said divisions(outsider/insider) to the harmony of the "One" cohesive relationship with the Celebrant/Funeral Director and Clients alike.

Offer that which is good enough and that you would offer to yourself principle. Be in tune with the natural unfold and the task at hand; with empathy for the mourners the deceased will be recognizable; have faith, it will come together somehow. Basically, the Ceremony must include; a birth to death potted history with personal attributes fitted in. Be sensitive on the type of questions to ask, also how long the eulogy should be with the overall scripted structure. Value the time you must put into it firstly. Others might not see the worth in what you might be or might not be offering and that would be adding to their loss; rather than assisting them through it. There is no such thing as a short cut to a worthwhile Funeral <u>Ceremony</u> !

What type of Funeral Ceremony Service(s) do you prefer?

A common practice in many cultures is to spend time with the body before the day of the actual Funeral service; this is a viewing that is also known as the wake and/or visitation. The viewing (Wake/Visitation) may be brief and take place immediately before the Funeral service, or may last for up to three days before the service. The Visitation also known by many as the "Vigil"; is held in the presence of the deceased prior to burial. For some the option for a wake can take place at the home of the family of the deceased. Some religions (Muslims) can opt out from the Funeral home altogether the last prayer over the body can be requested to take place in the decedent's home prior to transportation to the cemetery.
As quick as the Coroner can come and/or medical official a quick interment can take place and the family can accommodate for all of the final paperwork. However not all customs have a strong hold backing from their community to help alleviate such burdens. Holding a viewing or visitation at a location other than the Funeral home; can still be made as an offer(at a low and reasonable cost) to help the family for set-up and transportation services. Vigils have commonly been replaced by Viewing times at the Funeral home/Centres; with members of the family who respond to the condolences of visitors. In these cases the Celebrant can be made most useful and within accordance to the religious or non-religious cultural practices. Normally at this time the deceased will be displayed with open/half open and/or closed casket. The casket can be fully open with a foot panel as well to make it show like a half open casket.

The Funeral Officiant & Ceremony

What type of Funeral Ceremony Service(s) do you prefer?

Go back to an experience of a Funeral you have attended. What do you remember? Anything specific, about the casket, flowers, music or transport method?
Do you remember in particular the type of Ceremony?
How did it stand out? Was it as a reflection of them or sadly, not as truthful as you preferred? Was it deep and meaningful; shallow and as if to keep up with appearances? Remember a non-religious Funeral can be what you would like it to be?
From a very brief "Reflecting" Ceremony such as a and/or during before "Removal" from the place of residence or the Funeral home and very brief Committal services; that can be held at the crematorium or "Graveside". The greatest compliment a Funeral Celebrant can have, is to hear from families or friends, of the deceased say: "mom or dad, would have loved that"; or "you described them perfectly". It is the Celebrant's role to publicly display in the story of the deceased person's life.
It is our civic responsibility to involve and remind the families of these words we speak were the very memories which created the Ceremony; thank them for any compliments pertaining to the occasion and tell them it was in their words you have spoken of.

The role of the Funeral Celebrant is to help a family say goodbye to a loved one; commemorate and acknowledge the life of their family member. The feeling of accomplishment is certain and only when we have encouraged the family to say goodbye; in such a way which suited the life of their member.

What type of Funeral Ceremony Service(s) do you prefer?
Reflectional/Removal Ceremony:

This Ceremony is exactly as how it sounds and can be held at either the home of the deceased or at the(where they are resting)Bereavement Centre. Family, friends, neighbours, colleagues, etc. gather to pay their last respects. It is a very brief Ceremony and can include a reading or two; finishing with a favourite piece of music or song. Anywhere other than these places; that would also include the place of death and on its way for a disposition, the deceased cannot be presented otherwise. In Ontario the deceased must be always under the care and fullest supervision of an authorized licensed agent; responsibly represented by a licensed operational body to perform these services. The Ceremony can therefore take place in all or certain places along the way. Alternatively the "Visitation/Wake" can take place at any time, before and/or after the Funeral service, and where the body is not present at all; to last for hours and/or even days. The Ceremony can take place at the Funeral parlour; a social hall and/or the families place for a more private gathering.

On the day of the Funeral

Some will have the service at the church with the body present and is regarded as the proper place for Funerals, no matter what the denomination. In other rural areas and townships, the Funeral/cemetery chapel plays a much larger role. Celebrants are a recognized trend with Memorials and Celebrations of Life; the accomplishments, often with specially selected poetry or music reflecting something of the decedent's tastes. Even with more traditional, Chinese Canadian mourners who insist on an the impressive Funeral; are opting for the Celebrant Memorial and Graveside service. Especially for their elderly who have lived a long and fruitful life; these Officiants, for some can even do the public speaking in their own Asian dialects.

The Funeral Officiant & Ceremony

What type of Funeral Ceremony Service(s) do you prefer?
Funeral & Committal Ceremony:

This is a Ceremony held at the home of the deceased, if it is to be a small Funeral or at the Funeral Director's "Chapel of Rest", where larger numbers of mourners can be accommodated. The Ceremony includes a welcome address, a eulogy, a time of reflection, and a number of readings. Following the Funeral Ceremony, the deceased would then be taken to either the crematorium or the "Graveside" where a Committal Ceremony would take place.

Committal Ceremony:

A Ceremony held at the crematorium or Graveside. This includes words about the deceased, a reading, the Committal and a final reading or words of comfort, finishing with a favourite piece of music or song. The Graveside service with the Committal to earth, historically completed with a symbolic toss of soil on the lowered casket, is the last act of the mourners. Lowering and closing the grave is left to the cemetery workers.

Interment:

A ground burial in ethnically and religiously appropriate cemeteries. Cremation(reducing the body to ashes by burning) is increasingly common in Canada; however is not a final disposition. Cremated remains can also be traditionally utilized this way and still remains a common practice for some Buddhists. The cremated remains have no laws requiring specific placement of deposits, and can be spread anywhere. Some people arrange for an urn, and some cemeteries sell niches in a vault for this purpose. The Scattering Ceremony will be also discussed a bit later on; as it can also be more relevant with and toward a Memorial service.

Interment :

Post-burial rites interment of cremated remains in a grave can also be accepted with the ecological going green movement. The "greening" of the industry is another recent trend, affecting everything from the wood stain used on caskets to reducing the gas costs for cremation. A new kind of preservative is being promoted to replace the formaldehyde that is used in the embalming process because of the longevity of formaldehyde and its impact on groundwater zones and on the soil in cemeteries. Some Funeral homes now cater almost exclusively to the green market. Cemeteries may be either private or public, though there are legislated restrictions on private cemeteries. A gravesite is regarded by law as a piece of real estate and a deed is issued for the lot. The "deed" is frequently a form of rental and not a complete transfer of title. Most cemeteries have regulations regarding tombstones, markers and even flowers; contemporary cemeteries often try to create a park-like setting rather than traditional rows of graves. Ethnic, religious and even sectarian cemeteries are common in Canada and have restrictions based on memberships.

Some memorial parks with special theme areas or ethnic gardens have been established across the country, and costs for their plots include(care and maintenance fund) a percentage for perpetual care. No set period is allocated for the bereavement process; traditional Jewish law specifies one week of mourning, after which reintegration with the community is enjoined. Mormons often initiate special rituals designed to elevate to a state of grace the souls of those who have died without being initiated into the faith. Various Orthodox believers have an annual day for remembering the dead, when the names of all the dead from the community are read, and prayers said, after which the family will visit the gravesite.

The Funeral Officiant & Ceremony

Interment:

There is much to be said about tradition and the has been superstitions past down from the past. Wouldn't it be nice to be more up to date in creating that which can be more believable to the experience you shared with one another; rather than a public superficial show? You can wear black until you feel its right to start wearing other colours; or you might feel that public recognition is not conducive to your grieving process. Psychologically everyone is affected by these traditional programs and whether we like to believe in them or not; however as mentioned before and a much more watered down version, could be more appropriate a Ceremony. Widows in some traditions, such as Coptic Christian, are required to wear black clothing for a year, at the end of which a Memorial service is held. Some Catholics adhere to the practice of holding a Mass on the first anniversary of the death and some have masses said for the deceased, but Protestants have eschewed this remembrance of the dead. Mausoleums may also be erected for some cultures(example Italians) who prefer to be distinguished in this way. Some Muslims have a Memorial dinner annually, especially if the individual was well-known in the community.
For most Canadians, the Funeral service is the last public occasion for relating to their deceased loved one. Similar to the Mexican and other places around the world, some Native people living in the Yukon and Northern British Columbia, built over their graves; small houses can be seen, surrounded by a fence and with symbolic offerings. Except for those who follow ancestral traditions, there is little overt link with the dead.
The Band when living on the Reserve can help with these financial costs. When a Will is left behind, a private grave visitation can serve to bolster the memory of the deceased (lives on in the disposal of the inheritance).

Green and Natural Burials:

According to the Green Burial Council and many Californian practices, there are 3 types: Hybrid; Natural and Conservation. To avoid legal complications and bureaucracy, the grounds are rarely consecrated. Often with no headstone, the legal requirement of marking each separate grave for the burial register can be left to a shrub, tree or even an electronic chip. Green burial ground staff can make the Celebrant feel most welcomed; whilst, explain their particular processes and idiosyncrasies. This one visit can generate business for us as Celebrants; should you be able to establish a common ground with the proprietors and founder? More favourable and in growing numbers are from the Western part of Canada, such as Royal Oak Park, in Victoria British Columbia;(7yrsAgo) started to accept the concept of Woodland Green Burials.

Eventually investors came about to collate such collaborate agendas; however in Canada unlike the United Kingdom and the United States of America Cemetery grounds have corporate franchised as well as with the growing numbers of crematoriums. A care and maintenance fund plan and provincial Board of Directors with set in committees to oversee these matters. Going Green initiatives and non-traditional and/or hybrid Ceremonies were never really considered as important. These unconventional methods of ecologically friendly Burials and Celebrant Ceremonies were previously not in the budget. As time is passing not only is Canadian Society of Celebrants coming to the forefront; but also the purpose for a "Green Burial Society". The "Canadian GBS" is also an advocate responsible in a growing numbers of approved certificated practices; as well as opportunities to promote these kind of initiatives. These approved certified places and service providers can be found in Niagara Falls and Picton, Ontario.

The Funeral Officiant & Ceremony

Green and Natural Burials:

From the West Coast it benefit proprietors to try and somehow salvage(GTA and horseshoe belt) the dying breed; who have been for the most part resisting any change in this(Ontario) direction. Compensating for any insecurities by creating limiting factors carefully placed. Anything that could potentially arise from controversial short comings can be avoided and properly controlled from all unforeseeable incompatibilities. In this way all founders can create a special team of Celebrants; uniquely subcontracted and hand picked for this vision. It is certain that in one way or another; this book is to reach out and into the hands of such uncertainties; rather to expand on Ceremony knowledge for their venues to experience. The reasoning behind it was, the consumer awareness cemetery/crematoriums in the Greater Toronto Area; would stand to lose not to offer. Businesses are just too busy trying to look after the bottom line. Seemingly enough, very low budget Memorial and Celebration of Life services, were cofounded in these places. It is tough enough to look after their own employees, let alone an under appreciated Celebrant and who truly might be worth more, than what they can care to value.

Why settle for a compromised position? Perhaps it can create a less stressful strategy and to allow a much broader and truly bespoke occasion; in conjunction with the wishes of the bereaved.

Canadian Society Of Celebrants is a growing affiliation that wants to empower with transparency, the choices we can make available and that is the only real trade off. Empowering minds that do not care for middle man and can as to mine from their very own businesses. Our community can grow to mentor and educate the collective and in this way strengthen their level of discernment. The only way we can become reliable is by relying on ourselves firstly; unbind from having to give consumers the "my hands are tied" and "unfortunately I can not do this for you" scenarios.

Green and Natural Burials:

The onus is ultimately yours to choose from desperation and work for someone else(mouse trap). This book is not in any kind of way endorsing to lean in one direction or another, that would be for you to decide. Rather learn from these tools of training ! Embalming too must be formaldehyde-free. To be considered, a return to the older Egyptian methods of practice; with essential oils that can preserve the body for up to several weeks. Biodegradable casket options(Eco Coffins), handmade burial shrouds and absolutely no burial vaults; it can be turned into a nature reserve or picnic site. The growing number in Ontario alone has expanded to a few dozen and spreading fast and furious across the country at large. As mentioned inner city "Traditional burial grounds have become full; they become sterile and the land is never going to be used for anything else. Natural burial grounds are cost effective from a maintenance perspective. They degrade very quickly and then you're left with an area of mini-green belt; with regenerated flora and fauna, not cluttered up with marble or granite memorials.

"But what about Cremated Remains?"

Cremated remains are mostly pulverized bone, that weigh around as much as the deceased when they were born. When deciding not to have a Traditional Funeral Ceremony service, a direct cremation can prepare the body for a columbarium and burial niche placement; as well as the scattering and a Celebration of Life Ceremony and much the same as it could for a Memorial service. Also here's a second chance to get it right. When the deceased is not present the options become more like the scattering of cremated remains; in that it can take place in an outdoor garden, the home of a close family member; or even at the beach; or similar location of special interest to the deceased. It can take place shortly after the deceased has passed away or even months later to facilitate guests coming from out of town.

The Funeral Officiant & Ceremony

IS A Memorial Service The Same as A CELEBRATION OF LIFE?

A Celebration of Life is a Ceremony that is typically held in lieu of a Traditional Funeral or Memorial service.
What sets these services apart, is the level of personalization and tone. Unlike a "Besboke Ceremony", A Celebration of Life <u>is not a somber affair</u>; instead, we find lots of laughter and storytelling. The focus is not on the death of the person, but on the joy that the person brought to others. It can stand alone as well as be an incorporated component of a more traditional service.
For some, the best arrangement is to hold a "Celebration of Life" and in concert with a Traditional Funeral or Memorial service.
For others, a separate stand-alone Celebration is more fitting.
There are no exact rules or procedures to follow during a Celebration Of Life service. It should be what you and your family are comfortable with presenting. You can choose to have a Religious Officiant preside during the service an hour or so, or you may do this yourself.

HOW DO YOU PLAN A CELEBRATION OF LIFE ?

Planning a Celebration of Life is much like planning any other gathering that commemorates a life event. The bereaved need to decide on the specifics(time, place, etc.); how to get the word out and what elements to incorporate. This is where the Celebrant becomes most useful to offer in these situations; their time or resources to undertake such an effort. The value of a Celebrant is multifold and musn't be underestimated. Anything can be included with a Celebration of Life service; unless your loved one had specific instructions before they passed, their instructions should be respected.

A Celebration of Life service can include:

A Brochure: From simple to extravagant, and can make for all the guests at the service as a lifelong keepsake. Make certain to add a large variety of packages to choose from, and they can be printed at home or easily and professionally at a print shop for your convenience.

Refreshments: It can depend on where the service is held, but light drinks or even a catered meal much appreciated.

Music: Can be played throughout the entire service, intermittently or only at the beginning(procession) and at the end(recessional). Recorded songs, Funeral songs; and/or live music and in the genre that would have been preferred by the deceased. Speakers: Presented by the Officiant to talk about the deceased, and anything that would be of relevance through poetry, verses, excerpts(as the imagination can possibly allow).

Video Slideshow: To outline the life of t he deceased from childhood and throughout their best and happiest moments.

Display Boards/tables: Copies of the video on DVD for guests as a keepsake. Photo and personal items of your loved one are usually displayed.

Memorial note-cards: Usually printed on a high quality stock paper, guests are able to write a note to the family sharing their favourite memories with your loved one. Afterwards, these notecards are put into a special memory bag or box and kept for future generations to read and enjoy.

Guestbook: Similarly to a traditional Funeral service, and where available to attendees to sign.

Balloon release: A common activity when a child has passed; launch them into the sky in unison.

The possibilities are endless; however the personality of the deceased and what they would have preferred must be well considered.

The Funeral Officiant & Ceremony

Family/Client Decisions When planning for a Celebration of Life:

Must decide on whether to have a Funeral or a Memorial service?
Will it be stand-alone or part of a more traditional Funeral?
What tone do they prefer(it can be sad)?
Their budget: How much can they reasonably invest ?
Financial constraints can help to narrow down their choices on the details of the Celebration(food and the venue).
A wise idea to estimate the amount of guests: An estimate head count can help to alleviate any unnecessary cost on selecting the right sized venue and refreshments.
When and Where: When designing a Celebration of Life the choices of venue can become unlimited.
How much of the Celebrant do they wish to make use of:
For many people, the idea of planning a large event can be overwhelming. In these cases, a Celebrant can help take the pressure off by helping the client work through the details.
Perhaps just to help write a Ceremony Script and/or officiate a certain segment of the event might require to stand as back up in case the speaker falters. The Celebrant can help with all and/or partial aspects of the Ceremony.
Deciding who will and/or would like to speak?
The bereaved and/or the client can ask specific people to share their thoughts or invite anyone who would like to offer an anecdote to speak. The Celebrant can be there to give them guidance on the type of story they would share. The Celebrant can also be asked to speak on their behalf. What activities can they include?
The beauty of a Celebration of Life is that it can be customized in anyway conceivable. What feels good?
Where did the deceased spend most of their time and with what? It could be as common as a group walk and/or a bowling alley. The important thing is that the activity is an appropriate homage to the deceased.

Is a Bespoke Ceremony a Hybrid ?

Prior to becoming aware of the value of a Celebrant; alternatively a direct cremation and/or burial became the only standard for those who opted from any service.
Much like A Celebration Of Life Ceremony that had become the hybrid version(right dab in the middle) between the traditional Funeral and Memorial services; a "Bespoke Ceremony" is the giving back of choice to the consumer. Canadian Society Of Celebrants aspires to grow, bring about and to educate; in the way the Green Burial Council have, with their cemetery incentives. As mentioned in this book, some cemeteries have designed Natural Burial Ground sections and do provide these options. Corporations have taken off in the same way as to imprint of there own design; the meaning to provide Memorial services and to their patrons in the giving back. These places have become "Hybrid Bereavement Centres"; that curate much on cemetery grounds and including flower bed sections, for the scattering of cremated remains. Many associations and sister franchising have amalgamated into one provincial legislative body. Conservation alliances are helpful and together with the blending of this back up from States side (that had its origins from the U.K.) formed into a well organized Canadian Green Burial; that advocates for a naturally sustainable future in natural death care. Whether it be from provincial corporate startups and/or national and continental; the movement must continue and for the sake of future generations to come. A Celebration of Life service can be small, close and intimate shared with only close friends and family, or it can be of a larger scope with extended family, business colleagues and the like. Friends and family are given opportunity to honour their loved one who has passed, although it is an approach that is less traditional and more personal it can differ from a Bespoke Ceremony.

The Funeral Officiant & Ceremony

Is a Bespoke Ceremony a Hybrid ?

A Bespoke Ceremony can be have a somber and very sad tone to it. To better understood, a Bespoke Ceremony will go the extra mile and similar to that of à la carte packaging; a sample will be given on(pg. 151) just how it can appear and from the contract it will reflect the same. As mentioned a Traditional Funeral can hold up until the final disposition of the deceased. These services can be broken off into many sections and as such will be the many segments of many Ceremonies that build the entire process.
When we have a Funeral service on the day of final disposition is normally the only one in most cases traditionally considered.
All the other part that go into making of the actual Funeral service might be over looked. A Celebration Of Life is just that one moment of a segment just the same as the Memorial can be.
A Memorial however starts to take on many segments of its own; as well and from here as Celebrants we must continue to provide.
Perhaps we are the Hybrid versions of Religious Clergy;
in order continue on and recreate what can be best fitting for our clients. Just like the Funeral staff, we too must see them through this grieving process and for as long as it takes to consider of our own imagination; whenever the need arises to perform these type of Ceremonies. The following is a great example of the value that a

Graveside Ceremony service can provide:

Excerpt snippet from an Interview Case Scenario to brief through!

Both uncle Richard and Jordan were Lieutenants for Peel Regional Police. Richard was the more the a social character to recreationally help facilitate the family gathering. All outdoor events, interactions and activities; he would involve himself with all of them. He was seen as a fun loving member to the community and his family. Colleagues from his work might want to attend; but it's more of a private inner circle gathering and that would include his friends. No uniformed or military veteran type of service is required and mostly a plain clothing event.

Rather a small intimate for family service and with no special regalia uniform attire. The gathering is to expect of less than 100 people; an outdoor event preferred weather permitting and with a contingency plan. Preferably the "Graveside Service Package". "My uncle was not an indoor person"; "he was an outdoor fun kind of man" and " their something about the outdoors, that would better to reflect"; "a Ceremony for his service as Graveside Burial". For music ~ "he loved violins and anything with strings; student instruments, such as: cellos and really good saxophone instrumental; with more of the strings kind of music".

He was a Buddhist and throughout intermissions from one segment to another a triangular bell will be incorporated(in with especially the Moment of Silence).

The Funeral Officiant & Ceremony

Client Copy:

GRAVESIDE FUNERAL CEREMONY

FOR

RICHARD JOHNSON

11 am

Saturday September 16th 2017

BURIAL (unfenced side)
St. James Cemetery/Crematorium
635 Parliament Street Toronto

FUNERAL CEREMONY for Richard Johnson

" Nam Myoho Renge Kyo" Chant: by Nichiren   Buddhism "

" Nam Myoho Renge Kyo"
was a 13th –century Buddhist monk upon whose teachings were enlightenment.

It is believed that the chanting of his name can transform and help to overcome suffering when focusing on these fundamental universal Laws of Oneness that can unite all of awareness into higher consciousness.

My name is Maria Arvanitidis. I have been selected to officiate the Ceremony of this Graveside service, for the passing of our beloved Richard Johnson. Thank you for selecting me to be your Celebrant for this event. I feel truly honoured to be given this privilege to speak on the families behalf for this occasion. With spirituality and that of Heaven; it has not a final destination. Rather to be at peace within thyself; is to find the stillness from which to rest on. All things through time disintegrate, and cannot securely lock into the stable accountability. Roughly ten weeks ago Mr. Johnson was diagnosed with cancer of the throat and as a heavy smoker it did not come as a surprise that it was malignant.
From that point on, he had decided to welcome death surrounded by his loved ones and at home receiving palliative care. Richard honoured the Buddhist noble truth; in that when we believe in things to last forever, suffering will become inevitable. Lieutenant Sergeant Richard Johnson at the age of 72, on Wednesday August 23rd had realized this truth more than ever before passing away peacefully.

The Funeral Officiant & Ceremony

FUNERAL CEREMONY for Richard Johnson

Richard in his later years became a Buddhist; for this reason a triangular bell was sounded to commence and signal thereby after and before each segment. Lieut. Johnson was survived by his oldest sister Jessica and two other sisters Samantha and Kylie.
With great love he leaves behind his nieces Carrie, Jennifer, Melissa, Deborah, Caroline, Ashley, Amy, Kelly, Rebecca and Alex. From the boys are survived his nephews Peter, Paul, James, Mathew, Mark, John and Robert. Along with but to name a few of those family and friends who have through the many years got to know him and really well.

The following read is by a Buddha:

" Alas! Nothing is permanence.
That which forms is bound to cease.
Be calm as the highest bliss.

Now, a still brief moment only
And impervious to decay this body
then it is laid as earthly compost,
awareness fled; as useless as sleep!"

~ a Buddha

Eulogy:

Born on November 1st, 1945 to Miss Marry and Papa Tom; they too have passed away a few years back and peacefully in their 90's. On this family plot here at St. James cemetery; Marry and Tom are here today to welcome Richard and whilst we place his body next to theirs. His wife Margaret who is survived and by him for well over 50 years and has not waivered by his side; she has remained strong to stand by him. Margaret and Richard were proud in telling people how they met; the two of them in their early 20s, downtown at the beaches and over a game of volleyball. It was love at first sight when they first met over a game of Volley ball just before the summer break; a cute little story to be told and included with different kind of friends where they were sectioned off in groups; and into teams of the boys versus the girls. The guys would let the girls win; because the losers would have to take the winners out and so that's why they let the girls win. After their first date; they started dating for about three months and then they got married on September 25 1967. 10 months later they had their first baby Robert; who is now just turned 47 on July. After Robert came Richard Junior; then there was Marissa and then the twins, Allan and Ava. His oldest sister Jessica had also married earlier that same year to the man that he would be working alongside with. Jessica had married into a long line generation of Police Officers and her husband Lieut. Jordan Smith is still working part-time, had thought of Richard at that time could do with a descent life and that he did. Richard and Jordan both became Lieutenants for Peel Regional Police. In Some points during their career both Lieut. Jordan and Lieut. Johnson had the pleasure of working side-by-side. Thanks to his brother in law Richard's occupation was as a Lieutenant; "Lieut. Johnson" From Peel regional police and was on duty for well about 40 years and has retired roughly 10 years ago.

The Funeral Officiant & Ceremony

It was a sad day when he had passed away for Ashley; Amy, Kelly and Deborah from his sister Jessica side who were there at his home and here with us today..

Ashley the eldest sister described her uncle Richard as the fun uncle to go with to the park or at the beach. To go swimming and teach them how to ride their bikes and rollerblade.
He was the fun uncle. Although both Richard and the father of these girls, Ashley included were police officers only their father was the disciplinary one at home. Mr. Smith who is here with us today, was more loving and affectionate; but it was in a very serious and stern way. Where as uncle Richard was more of a second father to his nieces and his nephews children; he also had become the social recreational aspiration for them all and he motivated them as a loving coach. Throughout the years
Mr. Johnson was seen from the majority of the rest of his family as a more social character. Recreationally helped to facilitate family gatherings for outdoor interactions and activities. In the eyes of his community he was a fun family member.

Although Richard had no affiliation to do with any military, he was a Sergeant. We proudly stand witness to welcome these men and women and in honour here at this intimate gathering of
100 remaining friends from work. Richard's brother-in-law has requested that a moment of silence be given with the Last Post Reveille First Call Response:

First Call 911 response team wants to dedicate the Last Post, for the Moment of Silence and Reveille.

The Committal words

Richard Johnson was an outdoor loving kind of soul and taking all things into consideration is why the entire service was held as such and kept as short and very intimate. Before we commit Richard's body to be laid to rest beneath the earth I would like to say a few departing words. He came from a Christian Catholic family that could best be described and the following comforting words before now we stand and in the glory of God's presence in the great outdoors let us begin.

I will now read an excerpt from the Ecclesiastes 3

To Celebrate the death and resurrection with our Lord and in the name of Jesus Christ to hold Richard's hand we send him off with the following to let him go but never will he leave our heart he will be remembered .

For everything there is a season, and a time for every matter under heaven: (KJV1901Ecclesiastes3:1)

A time to be born, and a time to die:

A time to plant, and a time to pluck up what is planted;

A time to break down, and a time to build up:

A Time to weep, and a time to laugh:

A time to mourn and a time to dance:

For everything there is a season, and a time for every matter under heaven.

The Funeral Officiant & Ceremony

We now leave the memory of Lieutenant Sergeant Richard Johnson in peace. With enduring thoughts and respect, we bid him farewell. May you find comfort in your memories of him and strength and support from each other.

The bell goes off to signal the music.

Bon Jovi ~ " Living On A Prayer" ~ Piano, Cello, Sax Instrumental music

Thank you,

Maria Arvanitidis  **PEERLESS MOMENTS**

For those who have witnessed the rise of Chapel service followed by a Graveside burial before. At a burial or Committal held at a cemetery after the main Ceremony at a chapel, the Celebrant can be as brief to speak no longer than 5-8 minutes. These services are mostly standing and can become distracting and restless.
The main part of the Funeral proceedings, including tributes, eulogy, readings have already occurred and there is no point prolonging the grief of the mourners. In the previous Ceremony Script sample there was no Chapel service and the Ceremony was approximately 22 minutes in length. It can be negotiable from somewhere between an à la carte to elaborate variation.
This will strictly depend on the price list and packaging perspective. In this case the Graveside package was only made in reference to the time allotted in, for scripted speaking and the prices from which to start. Remove the musical entertainment and (Moment of Silence) the "Celebrant Speaking" is 10 minutes.
You might also take into consideration all that has gone into creating a well meaningful script ?

Elaborate and or Unusual Services:

The more elaborate Ceremonies haven't caught on as of yet; rather the budget is more the determining factor on these type of services. Bespoke Ceremonies must be experienced some more and they too will become traditionally accepted for the value that they bring. This book would like to enlighten the reader on the value and just how well received it can be to suggest with a traditional one. The size of the service as well as the personality and lifestyle the deceased can make the choice much easier. The location of the service is generally not the same as a Traditional Funeral, such as in a church or Funeral home. When directed by licensed agents to a loving resting place and while the deceased is in transit, from one licensed establishment to another; a variety of reasonable venues can be made to accommodate for such a celebration.

The Funeral Celebrant's role in this instance is:

When the Chapel Ceremony is complete; the Funeral Director will summon the pallbearers to come forward and take their places by the casket. The Funeral Celebrant will then lead the cortege from the chapel to the waiting hearse. When the Coach arrives at the cemetery, the Funeral Celebrant leads the cortege from the Coach to the grave, together with the directing Funeral agent. Another Ceremony can involve a Scattering of Cremated Remains Ceremony and/or the pouring of sand on the casket at a Graveside service: traditionally a container of sand or peat is made available for mourners to scatter over the casket as it is lowered. This act may be important to some mourners and those that like the ritual. The bereaved might wish to have this kind of ritual performed; you must liaise with the Funeral Director in order that the necessary materials are at hand.

The Funeral Officiant & Ceremony

Elaborate and or Unusual Services:

It seems to be Clearly misunderstood that there are only Memorials and Celebrations of Life For the Celebrant to offer. How would you like to start by categorizing all your packages under these umbrella terms ? As mentioned a Chapel service is with the deceased(closed casket)present and might not be a happy moment to Celebrate, what then ? The Funeral Ceremony must become a bit more elaborated and this is where the restricting misconception can come in? The clumping in of Ceremonies to best describe for the consumers needs has in fact become the standard.
Memorials have taken on an umbrella term meaning that can confuse the consumer; rather than elaborate to further bespoke the aspects of Ceremony and full expression that can be created.
On the other hand a more imperviously agenda are the Memorials publicly held for more than one deceased and clumped under the very same term. Perhaps a Chapel service without the body present? Whether it be personal or impersonal a Ceremony allows for the friends of the deceased to say farewell. In part due to the absence of the body, a Memorial Ceremony's emphasis is automatically transferred from the body to the life of the deceased. A Celebration of Life can make all mourners feel a real part of the service. These types of Ceremony are where Funeral Celebrants can come into their own; as they are not necessarily constrained by religious/traditional dogma. It is paramount that you work particularly closely with the Funeral Director and convey any wishes that may not have been discussed at the time of conducting your clients Funeral arrangements. There are obviously cost considerations involved with elaborate arrangements.

A Memorial Ceremony/Memorials:

A Ceremony held in honour of the dead. What do you think of when you hear the word "Memorial" ?
Perhaps a Cenotaph to congregate annually around and place a wreathe; and/or lay our poppy down ? This is an umbrella term and that can mean: a Funeral Ceremony when the body is not present; a religious service held in memory of the dead and at specific intervals after the Funeral; or it may refer to a public Ceremony Memorializing a public figure; or an event in which more than one person died. Whatever it may be it always is about remembering. A Memorial Ceremony is a service where the body is not present. It is an occasion that allows everyone to say goodbye. It is important to acknowledge the life of the deceased and to help the family and friends accept that their loved one is no longer with them. All present have the opportunity to say goodbye, with love, peace and dignity.
 Reasons for a Memorial service can also vary in the sense of the deceased being present as cremated remains or in an urn. As cremated remains have not had their final disposition a Columbarium service and/or the placing in a niche as well as a burial for a Ceremony service. Rather never been considered before because of it's umbrella term the many services are clumped together and that are not necessarily the same.
In technical terms a Memorial service can be a Funeral service but not necessarily agreeable to that of a Memorial Ceremony. Sometimes this kind of service can be called the "Scattering of Cremated Remains Ceremony". When a death occurs under normal circumstances, the body is usually laid to rest within a short time. However, when bodies cannot be found, a service without a body can be conducted. This situation can arise in times of war, tragic accidents and freak circumstances.
This service has much in common with the Memorial Ceremony but with a difference.

The Funeral Officiant & Ceremony

A Memorial Ceremony/Memorials:

Family and friends can be urged to Celebrate the life that has been lost, challenging them to focus on what they gained from knowing the deceased, rather than what they had lost. These services are not usually time restricted, unlike burials and cremations; many people can contribute to the Ceremony(subject to consent from the family of the deceased). It has been known for these Ceremonies to go on for hours. After the Interring Ceremony or burial at sea, and/or donation of the body to an academic or research institution, and/or the cremated remains have been scattered. It is also significant when the person is missing and presumed dead, or known to be deceased though the body is not recoverable.
Memorials can be individuated or become more public in their meaning of events and where more than a few deceased are reflected on. They can be festive and or very sad and somber. These services often take place at a Funeral centre; however, they can be held in a home, school, workplace, or other location of some significance. A Memorial Ceremony can include speeches(eulogies), prayers, poems, or songs to commemorate the deceased.
Pictures of the deceased and flowers are placed at the altar where the deceased preferred to be. After the sudden deaths of important public officials, public Memorial services have been held by communities, including those without any specific connection to the deceased. Memorial Ceremonies can follow an almost identical format to a Funeral Ceremony at a crematorium and without the deceased's body being present.

The Initial Call and the Interview Checklist:

The initial call as mentioned in chapter one is the First call. The following are some particulars you might want to address over the phone; This way they can as well as you be more prepared. What type of service were they looking for ?
What form will the service take; will it be semi-religious or strictly non-religious? You might have to go over what you offer with packages and pricing? Is it going to be a formal affair which will follow all traditional rituals or will the approach be somewhat relaxed with a more casual feel?
HOW MANY FRIENDS AND FAMILY MEMBERS WISH TO PARTICIPATE ?
NEED TO BE ADDED TO THE CEREMONY SCRIPT.
They might have to get back to you on "when" and "where" is most suitable for the arrangements to be made and go over all the alternatives.
"WHERE DO WE MEET" to discuss the Funeral Ceremony arrangements ? The meeting can take place anywhere that is of a convenient address and is completely up to the purchaser. Perhaps it can be suitable to arrange to meet at the Funeral/Cemetery Centre and/or at the Director's Office. Make as many options as possible to reach out with them in person; however it can also be arranged to converse either by phone or via Skype.

IS THERE A EULOGY GOING TO TAKE PLACE ?
IF SO HOW MANY SPEAKERS ?

Is it possible to KNOW AHEAD OF TIME AND HAVE ALL COPIES BEFORE THE COMPLETION OF THE CEREMONY SCRIPT.

The Funeral Officiant & Ceremony

The Initial Call and the Interview Checklist:

HOW MANY SPEAKERS ? AND ARE ANY OF THEM WISHING FOR ME TO READ OUT THEIR SPEECH ?

After establishing a time and place remind them that it could take anywhere up to 1-4 hours and to have nearby as many memorable photos and other pertinent relics; as well as most recent photos and especially hand written things, books excerpts/ poetry; whatever else they might want to bring up for conversation. The Funeral establishment can also provide a suitable and quiet space. In this case, perhaps a few telephone calls will further satisfy for collecting information. Voice over internet protocol is also worth asking the bereaved and on their level of comfort; that they would be able to provide all the(same as a home visit) details from home.

During these calls/texting and/or on line presence, a Memorial Questionnaire can be made available. It is very important however to establish "TRUST" during an immediate loss, to reach out and personally make contact. It is a critical moment for your presence to be felt; especially during a Funeral service where the deceased will be present.

Chapter III

During The Interview: "Helping To Create a Portrait"

First impressions are vitally important for any meeting with new people, especially for a Funeral Celebrant meeting a bereaved family for the first time. You are in effect a complete stranger coming into their lives; asking for very personal information and at a time when they may feel very vulnerable and emotional.
Gain their trust through your professionalism and sincere empathy, you will be enabled to gather a wealth of information to prepare for an appropriate and unique Ceremony.

The Interview Checklist/During the Initial Meeting:

Let not the first statement that comes out of your mouth be "*I am sorry for your loss*"; rather the following statements are but a few suggestions for a smoother transition into opening the conversation:1)"*Do you miss her* ?" 2)"*What was she like* ?" 3) "*What are you going to do now*?"

The following checklist is a useful guide; however do make notes of other questions you need to ask. Sometimes more clarification is required to use in the speech that may be missing about the deceased; do not hesitate to reach from time to time and check in on the family and/or Funeral Director. You need to talk to the family involved; in particular you need to talk to those family members who are arranging the Funeral. You will be able to adjust your role and the type of texts to use by drawing on the scripts and other resources you must research(could google translate some words to best fit your client needs that may not be English speaking). Sitting down with the family and talking about the deceased; is crucial; get as much information about the deceased as you can. Remember to make notes of anything relevant that you might be able to use. What music, (if any), has been chosen and at what point in the Ceremony must it be played?. Generally speaking there is time for three and/or two pieces of music and a hymn or live recital. Do the family intend to have an order of service sheet/booklet? This might be something that can be collaborated with the Funeral staff in charge of this service. This is how we learn, then as someone with little or no experience; it can place extra pressure on us to come up with such demands.

The Funeral Officiant & Ceremony

The Interview Checklist/During the Initial Meeting:

The design and print can also be of great help to us when coming up with the Anatomy of The Ceremony and/or "Vice Versa" for the Funeral Agents to collate in this manner. It also means, that whatever course you set for the proceedings to take place; you must commit to provide. The only suggestion we can offer you in this case is to use a printing company that guarantees same day or fast turn around printing. This will at least take the pressure off and allow you to properly prepare the order of service without being too rushed. Go and introduce yourself to the Funeral Director.
She or he, will not only be able to give you a few tips, and offer some valuable information will be gained regarding these specifics of officiating and exactly how to act. The platform must be built on the comfort that only confidence can bring for any given venue.
At specific points these options on how to proceed from that point on, can clear away the many pitfalls from our doubts and be they replaced with inspiration to experience appreciation.
The initial meeting will allow the Celebrant to further expand from the "First Call". Introduce yourself and briefly explain your role.
 Eventually we will come to feel more comfortable as Information Gatherers/Grief Counselors to Organize with Confidence; sensitively comfort listen and empathize. The type of Ceremony must be confirmed; don't worry, it will start to make more sense and on what might be a better fit soon enough. It is important to have a picture and/or as many pictures of the deceased during the conversation; a photo album can bring up memories as well.
You are there to collect details about the deceased's family, friends, school, work, hobbies, likes and dislikes and anything else that the purchaser(s) would like to include about their loved one.
Go over and discuss any particular readings, music or prayers that they might find from your collection and/or any other that preference to be included.

The Interview Checklist/During the Initial Meeting:

Be more thorough and detailed, the interview checklist is merely an aid to gathering the information. Alternatively you are likely to need to ask questions of the bereaved that refer to fond memories or anecdotes; In this way the atmosphere might become more uplifting as well as providing you with more valuable information. a solid background understanding of the deceased through the interview, even if you do not use all the information virtues and achievements and even exaggerate them which is fine. Rechecking details you forgot to ask for or note down some particular information can and does happen; do not worry, you can in the first instance contact the Funeral Director, who may have that information. You can also contact the bereaved, be honest with them, apologetic and ask them for the information. You may find that they offer even more information that will help you compose the ceremony; as well as making them feel more a part of the process and as an aid for their grief. The questions of the bereaved that refer to fond memories; virtues and achievements or anecdotes as well as providing the Officiant with more valuable information.
The more information we have of the deceased during this interview the better understanding and a solid background can build for a better script; however helpful not all the information will be imparted.

The Funeral Officiant & Ceremony

Bereaved Initial Interview Checklist:

It serves as an effective "aide memoir" for you in the preparation of a Funeral Ceremony. You will find that the checklist will be somewhat redundant to what the Memorial Questionnaire already asks from you as it will give you a better opportunity to fill it out more accurately than perhaps before. Rechecking Details ! Bereaved – Initial Interview Follow whatever direction the bereaved lead you and yet return to the interview checklist to address any gaps in your information.

CONTACT FOR BEREAVED:
Name
Address
Email
Phone
CEREMONY FOR:
AKA: *Ramsey*
Place, Date & Time   /   / **Saturday**   10: a.m.   *Perley&Rideau Veterans Health Centre*
Funeral Director   Other(**collaborative Authorities**)
Location: Cemetery/Chapel/Crematoria/Hall/Centre   *Beechwood National Military Cemetery*

Type of Ceremony:	

Wake&Visitation/FuneralChapel/Benediction&Committal/Memorial/Tribute/Graveside

Celebration Of Life

BIRTH / DEATH DETAILS:

Date of Birth *1930*   Date of Death *2014 / 12 / 24*   Age

Place of Birth *Scarborough Ontario*

Circumstances *Old age*

SPOUSE / PARTNER :

Name   Age

Where Met   Date

Where Married   Date

The Funeral Officiant & Ceremony

FORMER SPOUSE / PARTNER :

Name	Age
Where Met	Date
Where Married	Date
OTHER:	

FRIENDS & RELATIVES of Deceased (CHIEF MOURNERS):

Great Grandparents:

Grandparents:

Parents/ Biological/Adopted/ Step-Parents:

Brothers /Step-Brothers / Half-Brothers:

Sisters / Step-Sisters / Half- Sisters:

ACIFC CSOC

FRIENDS & RELATIVES of Deceased(continued) :

Children/Step-Children

Grandchildren

Great-Grandchildren

Close Friends

Others

EDUCATION:

Primary

Secondary

Further

Higher

Qualifications

EMPLOYMENT / OCCUPATION(S)

	From :	To :
	From :	To :
	From :	To :
	From :	To :
	From :	To :

HOBBIES / INTERESTS / ACHIEVEMENTS / REWARDS:

MILITARY SERVICE:

YES / NO

Awards / Medals: 1990 Silver Wolf award from boys Scouts

Details: Deputy Chief of the Defence (35years in Uniform)

LIKES / DISLIKES:

HABITS (GOOD / BAD), IDIOSYNCRACIES:

The Funeral Officiant & Ceremony

DETAILS OF PASSING:

Home / Hospital / Hospice / other

Thanks to carers?

OTHER RELEVANT DETAILS:

CEREMONY PARTICULARS:

Music:
    On Entry

    Reflection

    On Exit

Timeframe:

ACIFC   CSOC

CEREMONY PARTICULARS:

Images: Photos / CD / DVD / AV / Power Point

Curtain Close: YES / NO
Catafalque Lowered: YES / NO

Faith Symbols Displayed : YES / NO

Ideas / Activities / Singing

Flowers

Special Theme/Dress Code

Donations

Special Thanks

SPECIAL READINGS / POEMS

1. *The Old Salt poem by Mac McGovern*

2. *In Your Honour (unknown Author)*

3. *Of Their Own Accord~Excerpt from "Scars of The Prophet" by Mingo*

4. *"A Tribute to Veterans" ~Jerry Calow*

The Funeral Officiant & Ceremony

OTHER SPEAKERS *His closest Veteran friends Eddy Brown and Bobby Miles*
WAKE REFRESHMENTS Where & When? Remembrance Book
PALL BEARERS
NOTES What will you miss most about............?

During the Initial Meeting/ The Interview Checklist:

The essential information needed is mainly gained in an unhurried interview with the family. Friends and relatives of the deceased gather around, take a seat and simply talk. Ask them for permission to record(reassure them the necessary use for a well prepared story of the person's life) and as you guide them along in conversation; listen and take notes. This main eulogy is further enhanced by reminiscences from family and friends, written out and timed(As a guideline, the celebrant eulogy could be 15 to 20 minutes. Reminiscences which follow could be 3 to 5 minutes.). The Celebrant (or designated person) must then go about the creative writing and carefully selecting the most appropriate quotes of poetry and literature.

During the Initial Meeting/ The Interview Checklist:

Every detail of the Ceremony Draft must be carefully rechecked with the family to ensure that it is accurate. The option of cooperation with the Funeral Director on what musical selections is available ahead of time, can make for a more practical selections and that of when specially chosen by the family. Be sensitive with every situation and ask questions such as: Where and when was he/she born ; do they have any brothers and sisters; parents names and occupations; childhood memories and/or ambitions; school history; achievements and qualifications; work history; children grandchildren; endearing and less endearing attributes; what were the highlights of his/her life ? Personality traits; hobbies; holiday's; favourite pastime. What made them laugh and what made them cry? These sort of questions should really get the family talking. The "Interview Checklist" and "Memorial Questionnaire" are designed in such an order; however mostly to help motivate for off the cuff remarks and anecdotal memories. Do not be thrown off, when it is not going in the same order as the check list; make special notes of these things and keep in tune of all the stories shared. Continue to also ask, them what they think the deceased would have liked to have been most remembered for? Don't forget to make a note of what they remember him/her most for. In particular look out for recollections that bring a smile or a laugh. When you feel you need more input then go back over your notes and start the conversation again; by referring to something previously mentioned. Ask them to elaborate on something particular that you think might be useful. Also ask if there is anything that they would like specifically mentioned, and do make sure it is mentioned in the right context. Ultimately, with compassion, sincerity and great care, the Celebrant and/or with accompanying mentor will be ready to officiate the Ceremony.

Approving the Ceremony & Transcript Delivery:

Often, the Ceremony transcript previously prepared requires to be modifying. In this case, explain it to the bereaved and arrange delivery after a follow-up call. It must be delivered in person when possible. Some Funeral Celebrants believe that every Ceremony transcript be viewed and approved prior to the Ceremony.
Some believe that the bereaved have enough to deal with and ask that they be trusted to do their job. Always inform your clients of the many options; because they might want to review the Ceremony transcript prior to the Ceremony. A transcript is really the only real guarantee that can be paid for ahead of time as a Pre-arranged Ceremony would. After all, the only real guarantee that a Celebrant can accept money for the services and product rendered.
Pre-planning the Ceremony script and especially when it is signed by the deceased after it has been approved, is a sure way of managing a "Bespoke Ceremony". After the person has passed away then it can be revisited for minor adjustments and revision. Unless the deceased had made it clear that they would prefer the same Celebrant to officiate the Ceremony; anyone can step in and perform. The Ceremony or anything that cannot be performed immediately within a reasonable enough time is not to be held accountable and therefore can't be expected to be paid for otherwise. When the time for each Ceremony arises for its need and only then it can be paid for; with the exception of the "Bespoke Ceremony Transcript"!

Modification of the Ceremony Script:

Modification of the Ceremony script will be required especially with a pre arranged package. Tweaking the script can be necessary in all circumstances for approval prior to the Ceremony. Explain it to the bereaved to arrange for a follow-up call when it is necessary to do so and that most often than not that could very well be the case. E-mails or online delivery might not be so effective; rather a personal hand delivery or postal mail is best and from a pre arranged script scenario (possibly when the deceased had been alive to recommend your services). By posting the transcript, you will see examples of accompanying letters later. What Questions Should You Ask? With so many facts, names and memories coming out at an interview, it can be easy to lose track of the outcome that you need to achieve during the meeting. As mentioned earlier, while it is important to be flexible and to allow an interview to "digress", is where the "Interview Checklist" can be helpful. Follow whatever direction the bereaved lead you and yet return to the interview checklist to address any gaps in your information. Prompt you own memory, ensuring you ask for the pertinent information. We will now go through some of the important facts you will need to gather, then look at the example interview checklist. Find out the decedent's full name, however, be sure to include any nicknames. Seek guidance from the bereaved as to the preferred name to use throughout the Ceremony. As some of the mourners may be unfamiliar with the decedent's nickname(s); the bereaved may prefer to use both full names and nicknames at appropriate times during the Ceremony. Where there are difficulties with pronunciation, seek guidance from the bereaved and write the place name phonetically in your copy of the Ceremony script.

The Funeral Officiant & Ceremony

Modification of the Ceremony Script:

Ceremony Particulars have been given in the sample templates (in the previous pages) and unless it is a pre-arranged script then Name and address of Funeral Director and establishment as well as all the other particulars of where the Ceremony is to take place will be given. What type of Funeral Ceremony (cremation, burial, memorial, internment). In order to properly conduct a Funeral Ceremony for the decedent's family and friends, it is important to collect their details; in this way it can be correctly referred to in the script from these anecdotes. Parents' names are a good place to start. Often first names will suffice when prefixed with their relationship to the deceased on their first mention.
Are the decedent's parents alive and will they be in attendance? Brothers, sisters, husbands, wives, children, grandchildren and great-grandchildren and so on. Partners (Husbands, Wives, Common Law, Civil Partners, Same–Sex Partners) are clearly important characters in the decedent's life story and can be important the story of their meeting. Often grandchildren and great-grandchildren have affectionate names for their grandparents and it can be very useful to mention. Also other previous long term relationships/spouses, step-children. Establish how the bereaved would like to deal with it and whether they are comfortable mentioning previous relationships. Do not avoid or neglect that perhaps others might not accept as willingly to public scrutiny and as problematic for the bereaved further down the line.

Modification of the Ceremony Script:

Be guided by the bereaved as how to refer to previous partners and offspring from those relationships. Friends of the decedent, are often as important or more important than family.
A special mention of a few close friends of the deceased to a flock of hundreds. Community and other affiliations Clubs, Associations, Ex-Forces Organizations. These connections may be an indicator as to the potential number of mourners in addition to the above. Be guided by the bereaved to form the narrative; from the decedent's education and schooling to their ambition and, achievements. All material can be made useful helping to set the Ceremony scene. A profound effect on shaping their personality can be found through their trade of occupation; interests, profession and/or hobbies. After establishing a rapport with the bereaved, ask them to describe the deceased. Perhaps a light-hearted, personal and emotional reflection can be shared and to include within the Ceremony script.
Maybe it was an elderly deceased played guitar in his younger days as a hippy and imitated Janis Joplin, shouting at the top of his lungs. Watched Jeopardy and looked like "Alex Trebek" or a deceased lady who was scared of heights and climbed Mount Everest. Find out if the deceased had and memorable good or bad habits or vices. An example might be a non smoker who occasionally pulls out a joint to smoke. Was the deceased an animal lover? This often evokes many smiles and tears in equal measure. Rather than adhering to a set ceremonial formula, discuss the possibilities with the bereaved and ask them for suggestions; other formats of expression or variations that may be useful elements within the script to be added in.
Remind the bereaved that it is up to them to decide what is an appropriate Ceremony; that we are there for them only for advise and to assist them in achieving this outcome.

What happens after the initial meeting?

After the meeting you will know the type of Ceremony and/or the many segments of the service you are to officiate.
This is the time that you sit down and write a first draft of the ceremony. During the entire process and any questions that require filling in the blanks is this reaching out connecting period; a final draft is either emailed or a copy is delivered to a convenient address. This gives your clients an opportunity for them to read through and make any changes to what has been written.
Simple changes can be made over the phone or email; sometimes a rehearsal and where a second arrangement to meet again is possible. Your client is entitled to make as many changes as they see necessary and up until the day before the Ceremony.
Nothing will be said that has not first been agreed upon and given the permission to interact with Funeral Director as well as the relevance of these time allowances and that of special requirements for the Ceremony. During a Ceremony service where the deceased is present the restraints are many on what is permissible to be included and under the limited space of time. Hymns and/or prayers and Scripture readings can be included; depending on the Theme that it can be religious as the family cares for it.
The religious content can range from all to nothing, (it is up to us to go over all and/or as many options) has already been discussed the preference of suitability. Remind and note down all the necessary people(close to the deceased take part) that can really add to the Ceremony. This could be by reading a poem/piece of writing, making a tribute or performing a piece of music. Maybe they might have not been present at the initial meeting; get permission to reach out to them and connect with anyone who is to take part in the Ceremony(make the best use of this time).

What happens after the initial meeting?

It is possible that someone else might want to deliver their own tribute; we must ask that we get a copy ahead of time and at the very least 24 hours before. When those who wish to be participants in the giving of the public speaking; we must allot them a certain limit and to ensure that we can keep within the time allowed to us. Also how much time will be taken up by a moment of silence and or music?

Music: The first piece is the "*entry music*"; it is played as the mourners enter the chapel. At this time the casket is already present on the bier and the mourners might want to come have a look, music is faded out, and the service proceeds.
Alternatively, the music could continue playing until such a time as the Officiant feels is appropriate and signals for the music to be faded out. The second piece of music is often referred to as the "*tribute music*"; usually played after the quiet period of reflection and remembrance. It might however follow immediately after the quiet period without an introduction; then be attentive to have it gently fade up to volume.
The third and final piece is called the "*exit music*".
This is played in the last and final part of the service.
Often at this time a piece of music is chosen that is considered to be a bit more lively and uplifting. This should be a longer piece as it will need to play for a couple of minutes whilst everyone is still seated and continue playing as you lead the family out and everyone else follows. More will be discussed a bit later on this topic under "Memorial Service".

The Funeral Officiant & Ceremony

What happens after the initial meeting?

Other Speakers: You will find that very early on in the initial interview, it will usually be established whether any family members of friends would like to speak at the ceremony.
As previously mentioned; the eulogy is at the central part of any Funeral Ceremony, a personal tribute from those with an intimate knowledge of the deceased is a great asset.
Many families are happy with the Funeral Celebrant presenting the eulogy; however, be open to encourage others to share their thoughts. Make a note of other contributors names; in order to facilitate you introducing them. Those wishing to contribute but are too scared of "breaking up", encourage them to write a tribute down and the importance of giving you a copy; in case they falter and you must step in for them. Another suggestion, in the event of there being more than one speaker or children wanting to contribute is to split the tribute among those wishing to contribute; the participants will not only feel that they are supported by you but also their fellow contributors.

Suggested Readings:

As the Funeral Celebrant always provide a number of example readings with you in hard copy format for the bereaved to view at an initial meeting. If the bereaved or potential contributor feel that they "couldn't find the words", then the sample reading could be offered by way of assistance.

A mourner might also decide to write a tribute and prefer for the Celebrant(you) or someone else to deliver it on their behalf.

MILITARY/ FALLEN FIREFIGHTERS & LAW ENFORCEMENT FUNERALS:

They can range from very traditional and public to private and simple, as well more modern. In this case as there are many customs; this book is likely to focus on Canadian.

Where the Celebrant/Clergy is positioned for its purpose to have any value in all of this; the following examples can be witnessed. To find these type of protocols and guidelines for "Military and Civilian Parishes" alike: much can be revealed on-line(Google/U-tube) searches with a computer; however this book is not to be in any way of such redundancy.

Further details can be made available during the extended course(upon request) and to all Canadian Society Of Celebrant members. A Military Funeral can have participating members of a military force and the first in line assistance. It can start with the reception at the church and forming up of the parade. For all intensive purposes the Celebrant in this case might not really be of any relevance. When the service becomes more of a private affair than public; in this case the Celebrant can be asked to Officiate fully or partially with other religious officials. The Ceremony services can break up in segments; have a religious official at the church and then the Celebrant for a "Graveside". Remember you are there to get along where others will not have any of it; adapt your behaviour to the traditional imposed conformity and as it may dictate.

In this case you might be the son/grandson and/or (grand)daughter; what an honour this will be to experience. Whomever you might be for the experience; you have resonated with interest and might already know a thing or two about the custom. The Pal is usually replaced with the Canadian flag to cover over the casket.

MILITARY/ FALLEN FIREFIGHTERS & LAW ENFORCEMENT FUNERALS:

Whether it be at a place of worship(where the white Pal is replaced with the Catholic one, or not); Funeral Chapel; Cemetery Centre and/or Legion Hall/Gymnasium and whatever other place; it is up to the family members. A Military Chaplain is always assigned to these cases; but again, it is left to the discretion of the family. It can be Catholic and/or Protestant; however the celebration might opt out from the regular full Military and very careful protocol. A Memorial service at a public venue can take place as well. The Celebrant must be expected to assist with the entire Funeral process and must see to it that of all the military proceedings follow in due accordance. You must be very confident; it takes a real go getter to stand up, reach out to gather as much information as possible. Military Memorial services will not tolerate mousy shy characters and must you adapt appropriately to the right type of Liturgy replacement (fallen in combat/by friendly fire/accident or natural causes) for these soldiers. Take the initiative to contact with the nearest base, and get the proper readings for the ceremony; as well to show up and be there for the next of kin; show your interest and that you care. Collaboration is key to your involvement and participation as you might have to be somewhat respectfully aggressive to get it going as well as tolerant; patient and most of al mindful. Military protocols commences when the deceased enters and exists the place of Funeral Ceremony service. The Celebrant must collaborate with the military plans and preparations; so that a proper celebration can take place. The Celebrant must be well connected with military acknowledgment involvement; by staying a few steps ahead with protocol, and so that it may not interfere with the Funeral Officiant's Ceremony Scripted service.

MILITARY/ FALLEN FIREFIGHTERS & LAW ENFORCEMENT FUNERALS:

Wherever it may be the Celebrant must officiate and to what extent; (in this case the Eulogy, is at the heart of your Ceremony Script) you will be bringing to replace the Catholic or any other Liturgy with. Most of the time these "Words of Remembrance and Praise" have been replacing all other spiritual expressions; that the family may value over and to opt out from such religious Ceremonies. This is where the doors have widened right open for the Celebrant. Like any other program, there are time restraints to limit for each member(3-5min.) and why the Ceremony can be broken off into segments. Where there is a Celebrant involved within a Chapel Service, the Funeral custom and order of respect is not always listed. These examples can be given during a rehearsal; or (might not be of our concern)as otherwise directed(casket with feet facing the Chancel and Head facing the pews): Where the head of the casket can be seen from the left will be the Honourary Pallbearers and from the right side looking left to the deceased is the "Next-of-Kin" and behind them the other official mourners(research; get involved&show some interest). Where it differs in this case is from the Honourary Pallbearers side(4-6) now in this case can be up to 8(or 9). Behind the Pallbearers will be seated more Insignia(legion emblem/shielders) and that of Bearer Party(headdress and their Commander); behind them more Military Mourners. Note this roughly as a simple layout; for a more elaborate setting: a Funeral Parade Commander; Parade Chief Warrant Officer; Escort Commander; Escort of troops; Guard Commander; RCRegiment Guard and troops; Band and Bandmaster; All Officiatiants/Clergy; Gun Carriage Crew/ Honourary Pallbearers Pall bearers; commander and Headdress Bearers; Insignia Bearers; Rear Detachment Commander with troops; Gun Saluters and Commander.

MILITARY/ FALLEN FIREFIGHTERS & LAW ENFORCEMENT FUNERALS:

A large amount of participants that can vary in the numbers to reassemble with and such these regular forces/Militia armories/Gun Carriage and ambulance/parade marshals and troops lined up outside waiting for the casket to be led out by all the Officiants/Clergy(you)and looking like an organized mad house, all under their command. Officiant(s) move down the isle to position five paces in front of casket; then honourary pallbearers and their legion emblem bearers and all others (seated in following pews behind them)must follow. Funeral staff /ushers must have a close connection with you; they will be signaling when your at all times. (the above example was adapted from the 10/01/15 "Chief of Defence Staff" Passing of G. R. M. and on September of 2018 had become "A Celebration of Life" Ceremony) The above information was strategically placed and as an application made useful for this course; to exemplify the study of a case scenario further.

The information given in its detail description is an over view blending(of probabilities); however in most cases partial information is the training required that we as Celebrants must face and the reality of learning, to go after the rest. Use discernment when faced with an apparent level of secrecy; most of the time it is because, the information is misplaced and/or lost. It is not your problematic agreement; of who does what and how things are meant to be.

This Ceremony is best done on cemetery grounds; the gun carriage will be waiting there along with all the other signifying protocol that would start off at the cemetery gates if it is not and upon this entrance. You are to participate where you are appropriated for; these procedures have a special kind of grief and bonding that is not like any other to comfort in their loss.

There could be many laypersons participating in religious liturgy expressions; some bearing flags others medals.

MILITARY/ FALLEN FIREFIGHTERS & LAW ENFORCEMENT FUNERALS:

There will be many who will wish to come up to the front to read and have their presence heard: musicians; Honour Guard members; ushers and other such spokespeople(in to add a bit of eulogy and/or "words of remembrance"). Lead the procession out of the Cemetery Centre position yourself in front of the gun carriage and/or (Coach)wherever the deceased is to be carried in for transport. Honourary pallbearers will halt on sidewalk, four paces between ranks, facing inward, and salute casket and this then ripples out through their ranks and remain at the salute until casket is placed on gun carriage. Perhaps at the cemetery is where the Celebrant can be found most useful and/or after during Memorial services to come?

All officers shall salute and hold salute until casket is secured to carriage. When at the gravesite you take up your position with the Honour of Guards; the gun carriage comes to a stop and casket is lowered off the vehicle. The entirety of the service might not even involve the Celebrant until it reaches the finally of the service and its Benediction might be the only thing and can be very well integrated with a Committal service.

Your part is always going to be much more easier than you can possibly imagine. Whatever legion of shield the insignia bearers will place a cushion with the medals on the casket.

To the left of the Celebrant, the family mourners and to the right, the Military Mourners; at the foot end the Primary Pal Bearers and you opposite side. Most of the time the ushers and or Funeral Directors have this burden of direction to help along and where everyone must stand and take their place.

In this way everyone has taken their position. A rehearsal does take place for most of these events so not to worry.

Then all will "Stand at Ease" and you will step forward. All will take their hats off with the exception of the guard and band.

The Funeral Officiant & Ceremony

MILITARY/ FALLEN FIREFIGHTERS & LAW ENFORCEMENT FUNERALS:

When you step back the service will be over and all head gear can be warn again. The Bugler sounds the Last Post; all officers salute until Reveille is completed. A formal procedure for removing and folding of the flag by the Honour Guard; who then presents it to the next-of-kin. A minute Guns will commence firing and then all others can come and pay respect at the foot end of the casket.
The Military (is not as harsh as one might think when it comes to burring their own)will help to assist with any religion family beliefs and traditional practices. Like with anything else, we all must move forward with the collective changes and that of public co-census. As Officiants we must learn to work with the paradox; because what may appear as a similar Funeral and Burial rite may not be so. Some customs pose few restrictions and others have very strict rules; to which the faithful are expected to adhere without question. Stay closely connected to these individual needs, it is not our place to judge. Make it your mission to provide a powerful service and meaningful in its request; just as long as it be with law of the land and the cemetery by-laws. The military will always be around; but certain faiths are changing and with bereavement support groups are helping to diversify from churches.
Religious representatives might be having it tough to adapt; because families are starting to prefer, with more modern ways of Ceremony, that the Celebrant can offer.
Be the creative solution and not as the limited(hands tied)problem. Anything is possible with "_imagination_" and can be recreated to best fit for your Ceremony preference. There are many online references available; however this overview is all about getting the reader to open up and from there, getting all others and in the same manner to be less fearful. Be it beneficiary and/or purchaser; the client always gets last say.

MILITARY/ FALLEN FIREFIGHTERS & LAW ENFORCEMENT FUNERALS:

Discover the reasoning behind "consistency" and find the trust in your own approval to design, what it is that we prefer.
As it was mentioned briefly and to point out, that not all Funeral expressions are alike. Firefighter/Police and all other Civil Servants Funerals and Memorial Services; can be as ripe with their tradition as the Military tradition. These traditions are designed to give the proper respect upon the passing of those and in so many ways have placed their lives at risk daily for the public. Fire department customs play an important role in honouring Firefighters who have passed. Full Military-style honours are accorded to those who die in the line of duty.
A bell service might be an appropriate part of and maybe the same "Placing of the right Glove" as might be done with a Police service. Keep it simple and just consult with family; because their wishes outweigh the traditions of the fire department, so while the fire department's family liaison should present all the options, the family can select only those elements of the service they wish to have included.
For example, tradition might call for an Honour Guard to stand watch at the casket during the wake or viewing; the family may decline for any reason. The family will be presented with all the options; but not be pressured into including a tradition simply because the department(or the chief) wants it, or "the public expects it". It is important to reach out to as many and/or all participants for this creative/collaboration also can be expected a rehearsal that you might have to organize well with.

The Funeral Officiant & Ceremony

MILITARY/ FALLEN FIREFIGHTERS & LAW ENFORCEMENT FUNERALS:

All of these decisions must take into consideration the final wishes of the deceased and the preferences of the family. It is not your responsibility to gather all the departments Honour Guards/Pallbearers, you are there for the rehearsal and or debriefing of it from the Funeral Director/Family Liaison and/or department. Your task is in the Ceremony Script and the collaboration of Officiating. You might be asked to Officiate at the "Vigil/Wake/Viewing/Visitation" or you might not.
As a Funeral Director does witness these Services more often than not; the Police department too will also have the Honour of such guards that rotate every 15 minutes or so(one at the foot end of the casket and one at he head) before the viewing and after.
A "Walk-Through" is a Formal Ceremony during the wake or viewing. At a predetermined time, uniformed members and dignitaries enter and pass single file by the casket.
You will be able to distinguish who the Colour Guards/Pal Bearers/Honour Gaurds are; because they will be the only ones who do not take off their head gear at and during service(as it is not proper to salute if you are not wearing a hat). Law enforcement officers also have strong hold on their pledge of unity and honour for their brotherhood. They put their lives on the line for us each day while on duty. Each circumstance again will differ slightly and like every other too this way is where the Celebrants can enhance these properties as well as respect the unity of uniform this way.
This kind of Ceremony can be as lengthy as to have rehearsal added in or just a higher police presence to be escorting in a lengthy procession of followers to the final resting place.

MILITARY/ FALLEN FIREFIGHTERS & LAW ENFORCEMENT FUNERALS:

Law enforcement Funerals are very similar to those for fallen firefighters and military personnel; however not always planned and according to Wikipedia a "Last Radio Call" Ceremony amongst the department of officers that gather; dispatch issues a call to the officer for a moment of silence and then a second call to after this silence announces the failing to respond in the line of duty. It may also be included into the Ceremony script; to mention of the officer's background, the length of service, and circumstances of death, or it may consist of a few simple words, usually ending in, "Gone, but not forgotten." Other common traditions for the "Final Goodbye" to a fallen officer may include a bell of peace Ceremony rather than the shots of fire at the Graveside service. At the interment, honours may include Last Radio Call, three-volley(firing 3blank cartridges) salute(or 21 bells), flyover, flag folding, playing of bugle/trumpet(at dusk), bagpipes, and a dove release. Traditionally the bell is swung 21 times to hear(them home) because it is the code to call home(10-21). Whatever the final wishes of the fallen officer were will take precedence and then the family. Find out what these Memorial wishes were and reach out for this connection by making contact with those closest to the deceased. Anything from the choice of music and to overall theme; these considerations must be consulted with the family, as well as with accordance to tradition and that of their own Memorialization for their loved one. In some cases it might be at another private gathering to hold as separate from this public Ceremony and at others blended into segments. Again if it were not made recommended by the actual deceased than their wishes will always outweigh the traditions of the department.

The Funeral Officiant & Ceremony

MILITARY/ FALLEN FIREFIGHTERS & LAW ENFORCEMENT FUNERALS:

In the case, where the family is first choice; than do not even bother with any other to connect and in most cases that is where you will be most welcomed and valued. A rule of thumb with this type of service and that differs from the military; is that less force is needed here and more with just the allowing of it to happen from their end. Only do what the family is asking of you and paying you for. Options can include a school auditorium, a civic auditorium, or a large church and does depend on the type of service.

The venue might be small and intimate and/or large enough to accommodate several thousand mourners and have a parking lot where the procession to the cemetery can be staged.

To Sample; <u>The Order of Service can be as simple as</u>:
A prayer→ Opening remarks/greetings→ Special music→ excerpt/poems → other speaker remarks→ Mayor→ elected district and federal official→ Family representative(s) → Union representative→ Department representative's friends Eulogy – Chief, dignitaries, and/or family→ Special music→ Presentations→ Closing remarks/prayer→ 21 Bells Ceremony (also may be performed at cemetery)→ Bagpipes play (Amazing Grace, for example)→ Final Radio Call Ceremony (also may be performed at cemetery)→ Colour Guard retires the colours→ Bagpipes play (Pallbearers remove the casket)→ Dismissal instructions.

There will be more examples to sample <u>The Order of Service</u>: in Chapter III with the Anatomy of the Ceremony; as well as, the benefits of a program booklet in this chapter.

A Moment Of Silence:

A Ceremony can be broken up in segments: from an elaborate start the night before to the next day Chapel service; followed by a Graveside(anywhere of 5-8/even 15 min.).The Chapel service can even take, well over a couple of hours(From deceased arrival to departure of the mourners). Roughly a 20 minute slot as a typical example and with the remaining time with music and other professional Funeral staff speakers as well as coming to the front to pay one's last respects. Remember, not everybody might feel up to giving a condolence or express in how they are feeling; and what that loved one meant to them.

Everyone has their own unique ties and journey through the process that they grieve. How and/or when is up to them and in their own divine timing to be present in this way sharing and speaking. The Moment of Silence is valued in this case the most and where it can be utilized within the Ceremony; so that it can be scripted in well for timing purposes as well. A well prepared script can go for up to 30-45 minutes and perhaps take into consideration how much time it can request or be added on to near the end perhaps for "A Moment of Silence". The moment of silence can be a great intermission for holding space to support this those who might be wishing to come up to the front and share their story. Depending on the venues time accommodations and ceremony script there of; that anything unscripted can arise from this and be encouraged and/or welcomed to join in. This Moment of Silence can adapt to help with flexibility and easy flowing of the Ceremony; however can also be preferred somewhere in the middle with music in the background or lyrics that everyone can relate to join in. Rather to replace by music also in the end it can be most welcomed to have a 20 minute script with 10 minutes of this kind of silence and anywhere after the introductions of the Ceremony are made to help with flexibility.

The Funeral Officiant & Ceremony

Traditional Symbols and Ceremony Elementals:

A lot was mentioned in the previous(as there is more to come) Military section; however it will not be further elaborated as to form redundancy and the choice can be left up to the student for further study. <u>A Guard of Honour</u>: can be quite spectacular and add a touch of theatre to the Ceremony; some examples can include: a motorcycles cortege, fire engines, sporting teams, and other such uniformed services. A popular means of expressing a tribute for the deceased who had a significant affiliation with such representative organization.

<u>Photos</u>: At the time of your first meeting with the bereaved; preferably a recent photo to ask for and/or a good photograph(s) of the deceased as they would to be placed later on the casket and/or by the head; at the front of the Ceremony venue and where ever else that they might choose a tri stand too. The bereaved often see this time as an opportunity to get the photo-album out. Just be patient and gently steer the bereaved back onto the interview structure.

At the actual venue there could be catering and other planning that the Funeral Director might help with(on what type of refreshments); venue, budget, and on what other constraints, is not your concern. As a Celebrant you are not the planner of deciding how to personalize the event let the family work this out with their Funeral Director and/or other planning caterers. Many people create a tribute movie or slide show and display photos around the venue. The choice of music and readings can also be highly personal. Although "<u>The Anatomy Of The Ceremony</u>" is strictly designed for us and will further be described; but not necessarily to be confused with the program book provided to the public.

Funeral programs are an important part of a Funeral service. They provide important details regarding the Funeral or Memorial service from start to finish. They include poems, obituary, photos and other relevant information.

Traditional Symbols and Ceremony Elementals:

The Anatomy of the Ceremony is exclusively made for you the Celebrant to keep synchronized. The Anatomy will help to set these order of events(this structure will be further expanded in great detail to place such events): as readings and music followed by some type of activity and then a reception.. There is no right or wrong way to do it. The theme will be appropriate to know and have included in the Ceremony as much as possible to also dress the part if that is required of us. The deceased perhaps did have particular musical artist, film, or set of characters that might be a request that attendees dress in costume. Remember, there are no rules. Let the Funeral Director and/or family decorate for the theme; your responsibility is to know the deceased was a collector, for example, and not how to decide to display some of his or her items on a special table. "Memorabilia", provides comfort to mourners to place selected items, of particular significance to the deceased, on and/or in the casket after it is lowered into the grave. These items can range from a teddy bear, favourite reading material and glasses, a machete, a bottle of Cognac, coins, a chocolate bar, jewelry (check with cemetery or religious restrictions on what can be placed). Offerings as well as actually indulging in traditional drink and food on at Graveside services as well as spilling expensive brandy/wine and oil are common practices as well. These "Written Resolution", can be expressed publicly to honour the deceased relationship with the Lord; a scripture or poem of resonance to and/or use a poem or prose that can express the words of how a person maybe feeling.

Another could be by putting together a variety of pictures of the deceased life to show during the Funeral or Memorial service.

The Funeral Officiant & Ceremony

Traditional Symbols and Ceremony Elementals:

Rather than a guest book the Funeral home might offer a journal to replace it and where these stories about the deceased in childhood; married life and career. Using a "Tribute Journal", the guests attending may share short memories or thoughts about the deceased; as well as story or anecdote that can be informal and light hearted.

<u>Prayer Cards</u> are traditionally very useful, (with a Bible verse, deceased full name, date of birth and date of death as well as a picture); it can serve as a great keepsake for surviving family members and friends. <u>Flowers:</u> The once popular wreath adorning of the casket has now been replaced by an arrangement of flowers, often with colours requested by the family. In a decorative sense, these arrangements can add warmth and expression at a solemn occasion. Some families and friends of the decedent's will bring flowers cut from their own gardens. The for the bereaved might also to request "family flowers only"; preferring the mourners to make a donation ("In Lieu of") to a selected charity.

Another attribute for ongoing seasonal events are Memory Stones, balloon releases; as well as the autumn or spring walks to remember and release balloons. The opportunity has not enlightened for such gatherings as of yet and to find any real value for a Formal Ceremony that any real Celebrant would perform; and unless some sort of payment can be put in place. Sometimes various charities will team up with certain Funeral homes and host an Annual Butterfly Release for a community gathering at public parks; followed by a picnic (providing light lunches).

Often the charity will be providing to collaborate with certain Funeral outfits that will offer the an online service pre-payment for the butterflies. What a great way to come together to laugh, cry and celebrate the lives of their client's loved ones with friends and family; as well as replenish the butterfly population.

Traditional Symbols and Ceremony Elementals:

Also these are Memorial events that started popping up in actual Funeral Centre/Cemetery grounds over the last 10 years to help families cope with the grieving process.
Monarch Butterfly release at a public park and/or cemetery grounds. Butterflies are fragile, beautiful creatures whose lives on this Earth are brief. Personalized candles are also special for a Funeral service as well as Memorials; it can be given to an immediate family member and with a specific theme and photographs. A Candlelight Vigil is another Candlelight Memorial service. Bereavement resources are well funded groups that can provide supported and much encouragement along the grieving process. This kind of Corporate program sponsored by a grouping of Cemetery/Funeral Centres is a great way of giving back to their patrons. Depending on the location for each and every one and will hold it at a different time; starting from November right through to before Christmas. A great way for the Funeral profession to sponsor and promote their management; that does officiate as well as fund alike the Clergy to collaborate a Ceremony with.
In this case it is something fairly new and well on its way to acknowledgement of the Celebrant in its category with Ceremony officiating. The paradox of who shows more heart and spirit; over another has never been the compromise and to cast for any judgment here. It is rather not the amount of allocated finances; as it is the placement of one's value and where it might be best fitting to support. Hopefully this book might wake us all up and to become more trusting in this process. They have discovered how to put together a Candle-lighting Ceremony and video tribute that includes readings, musical interludes and reflections.

The Funeral Officiant & Ceremony

Traditional Symbols and Ceremony Elementals:

This is a paying of respect for the patrons who have lost a loved one and after they are given a poinsettia to take home for Christmas. The giving of an ornament to place on these trees of remembrance and the list of giving back to the community in this way is the greatest business gesture in showing that we care.
To give this kind of space and dedicate a Ceremony service requires not just light refreshments but in its tasking measures to hosting such events. A great step forward to consider by the Funeral staff professionals; to welcome all referrals and have them contact by telephone and/or email to RSVP for seating.
Then be it arranged with an Officiant of their choice.
Reflecting on the images that can best represent as messengers their followers. Whatever the connection is in a most collaborative of pastoral services; great management will have their feelers out and on these exact preferences. After all, the mourners are potentially our future paying clients. Like any other client, allow the management to be involved and earn their trust; that they are in control at all times of the entire situation. Adjust to whatever idiosyncrasies these venue organizers have; connect with their best interest at heart and at the level that reassures themselves in secured comfort. Learn from their "Business Savvy"; Funeral Directors can come up with the entire service program and so it would be very wise to let them. Allow for the important players to feel it so this way. In their establishment and just like every other venue, let it simplify as it unravels. Sometimes the more we can allow the organizers to participate, the easier it can be. The Anatomy Of Ceremony will better describe these responsibilities. You kind of get the overview as the etiquette is similar when dealing with Firefighter funerals and Memorial services; however we all play an important role in honouring our proper respect.

Traditional Symbols and Ceremony Elementals:

Memorials will be further discussed as they too can be on a multiple scale celebrated once a year and on a massive scale example: "November 11". This commemorative application with the laying of the wreathes for all War Veterans and visiting the various monumental Cenotaphs to honour the dead, by laying down their poppies. All proceeds go to Veteran Charities, when purchasing a poppy and a wreath to lay down. This is "Tradition" at its best remembered ! Roadside Memorials are also a good way to express with perhaps a cross and/or ribbon. Sometimes if it is a person riding on a bicycle that meets their tragic death by a driver; we might see ornamented a bicycle; other times and mostly our pets might be found this might be the way it all first started on our very first Pet Ceremony. With violent, unexpected deaths, memorial symbols or elemental ornaments will help not only to remind us; but serve as a warning for more awareness to perhaps our blind spots and where it is that we need to be more safe. These are the markers(Law of the land permitting and within reason)found at the side of a road; in around construction sites; highways and well just about anywhere accidents can and do happen. Other more elaborate ones are little houses that look like small propped up churches; a lit candle is in place, all around the backing of these walls religious icons and pictures of the loved one. From decorated stones to statues they will tell their story somehow about the deceased and their fatality. Some may choose a casket with their own cultural designs; especially if the Ceremony includes an open casket. For many years it was customary for friends and relatives to buy flowers, and the size of the floral spray varied according to the relationship with the deceased.

Chapter IV
Sundries & Disbursements:

To recap(tying up loose ends from previous). Any miscellaneous objects from "Traditional Symbols and Ceremony Elementals and/or What is the relevance for a CONTRACT"; are some various encounters we can face, as third party representatives. Also, that good old question of: how much must we be charging? To point out, as Celebrants we might be considered in the Funeral service Contracts under "Disbursements". When Funeral Homes write up contracts, their relevance will be as financial investments; that is further grouped into a trust fund pool and/or insurance. Prepaid third-party expenses as they are known; do not have to be guaranteed and why it was discussed previously to create our own. Few establishments do have Clergy/church service estimated price; but it must be broken down in detail and be guaranteed.

This is why(from their end)it is preferred at the time of need only, to include a Ceremony. At this moment there is no pooled in and under a separate account trust fund for Canadian Society Of Celebrants. This type of trust fund is designed for all licensed Funeral establishments within Ontario the privilege of deposit entitlement. Perhaps in future a collaborative agreement can be reached to include in this investment the Canadian Society Of Celebrants and for its members to report annually such prepaid funds. The Funeral, Burial and Cremation Services Act requires this from all Funeral establishments and under the licensing body of Bereavement Authorities of Ontario. Funding certifications are provided from these establishments; that they must then fill out for their clients to report; under either an insurance claim and/or trust fund claim, when entering into a pre-paying contract.

For now all Canadian Society Of Celebrants members must take into consideration and independently as acting third party entrepreneurs.

Various Encounters:

Celebrants encounter many different situations with bereaved families when preparing and conducting for these types of Ceremonies. The experiences will always have their opportunities for growth and from these unpleasant circumstances we are there to be unbiased.
We must always conduct the Ceremony with compassion and expertise. What might be some of the strategies that you can think of using and when dealing with difficult family members and/or friends? Words can never be enough to soften the shock and pain we feel when someone close to us dies. People have their own unique individuation to grieving; the range of emotions are too many and intense.
Tones of sorrow; anger are displayed; displaced blame, pain or hurt; the disbelief can be crippling and can cause a reluctance for them to speak. During these moments the attempt to keep a normal composure can have many blowing up in places where they never could imagine possible. It is so easy to become triggered and fly off the handle; irritable easily aggravated; not very tolerant and short tempered. The extreme nature of these expressions of grief can lead to mourners behaving in particular ways. Difficult situations can arise at the Ceremony and you are not there to be any bodies savior; rather be mindful, observant and forgiving. "Hostility" between mourners and/or family of the deceased as well as that from societal grievances toward the deceased from previous; these circumstances will not always change the situation.
Kindly remind them why we are here; allow the mourners to sort and address these issues amongst themselves.

The Funeral Officiant & Ceremony

What is Leadership:

Can you start with today as the day that changed everything? What would you choose to keep and what would you choose to leave behind? What would you do to ensure you were happy, and moving closer to your dreams? What excuses, behaviour, people or self doubt and negativity would have to be discarded to change your outcome and outlook; how would it feel to no longer need to carry all that baggage? When we think that someone is against us they might just very well be promoting and out for themselves. Mostly those who lead the way for others are doing it for themselves; rather they are not going to wait around for something to get done, they either move on to something else, or get it done themselves. Are you someone who can speak from your truth, set boundaries, trust your instincts, follow your heart, and advocate for yourself? Do you believe that you already have the answer to your question? Just listen, believe and act on it; instead of deflecting, excusing and sabotaging. How easy is it for you to say no to do what you need to, or feel, or believe in; without getting pulled down into feeling guilty and that you might have alienated another? When given the opportunity to take the risk and learn, will you do it; or are you just a people pleaser, afraid of making a mistake? Every opportunity is there to show us something and how long we choose to stay with it is up to us. Could it be also that the best leaders make great followers ? Not everything is based on theory; however the opportunity to follow certain traditional values; does a good leader make and perhaps to find best fitting as to represent its("Lest We Forget") fallen. Full military-style honours of passing heroes who have died in the line of duty and their relations; just remember you are not there to steal the spot light from anyone. How to be a public speaker will be elaborated upon and as mentioned in Chapter IV.

<u>What is Leadership</u> (*to be continued in Volume Two*)
What Funeral professionals forget and sometimes only an Embalmer can remind them of, to be the wiser, in that; the "<u>celebrity is the loved one</u>" that we have lost and not so much the Funeral representatives; nor the family and/or friends, who come up to take the stage and speak. This is the number one biggest fear we hold and why we shy away from; as well as who we do allow to represent us (so they do not attract for any fame or fortune from the unfortunate event) and such misfortunes as to lose a loved one, in this way. It is a very touchy matter and to why it is the reason behind, who gets to be visible to represent the Ceremony; as well as speak on the behalf of even management ? Trust is so important and familiarity breeds trust. These are some qualities and attributes of integration for the many to adjust with and from all the many fears that hold; not only the rest of us behind, but most importantly themselves from taking charge. This topic however is altogether on leadership credentials. Maybe it's time to start acting and believing that today is that day and start taking action. So can you stand strong and appreciate your own unique gifts, talents and beliefs; while still being able to appreciate others, and support their magnificence without jealousy or judgment? Do you have the empathy and compassion for yourself to acknowledge the well deserving praise from time to time and nurture yourself, where others have never been able to? When deciding where to put our energy, effort and passion; do we do it for our own integrity, circumstance and awareness ? Can we support, commit and be loyal to that we honour and believe in; (not to undermine others) to show the world who we are, what we care about, think and to let them know where we will bend but never break? A good leader must be who they are and realize that they can live up to their own potential. Dare to dream the best version of yourself that only you can be and support others to do the same!

The Funeral Officiant & Ceremony

Gaining Trust:

Maybe you have never met the bereaved before and their voice as sounding unfamiliar when first engaging in a conversation. Express your condolences and explain what part you will play in the Ceremony. Ask for their cooperation to make them feel part of the process. Reassure them that they have ultimate control and that you will work "with" them to produce a fitting Funeral Ceremony for their loved one. You will know early on in the initial interview their level of confidence and just how accepting they might be for them to establish a trust in you. The bereaved might be so overcome with grief, be supportive and tell them that "you are there to listen, when they are ready share". For them to start expressing from their many memories; it might break down some grieving barriers for them and can effectively provide you with material for the Ceremony.

How Much Can A Celebrant Charge?

Funeral corporations/homes have had for many years the option in place and from their pricelist packages; such services as "The Celebrating of Life" Ceremonies. Over a decade ago, these Ministries would have charged at very least $400(pocket money). The "brotherhood" was far too kind and perhaps(now in 2020) the doors have opened(to subcontracting) much wider; to accommodate other such and non-ordained equivalent opportunities. Identify what prices your local market can stand; more importantly how does it reflect from the purchase of the overall Funeral services and products? Prices can range for the services of a Funeral Celebrant as they might wish to freely interpret. Sometimes people can be on financial assistance and for this a Budget Ceremony could be considered. A pretax deduction of 15% is considered for corporate affiliates and/or small business owners.

How Much Can A Celebrant Charge?

For most ordained occasions, a stipend fee as Honorarium, is handed out to Clergy all across the board; but truth be told, when making over a certain annual amount, an HST (HarmonizedSalesTax)number must become more relevant in these matters. For a Standard Ceremony it musn't be too much more than the above considerations and that would accept or offer of such services(net income). Again with the more elaborate Ceremony it can get more complicated; the more time that can be invested, the more work can be involved. Not to be too obviously rigid; however it will start to make more sense as you read along further and might to catch up on this topic.

Collaboration:

In the same way that gender and racial inequalities of who is best qualified to conduct a Funeral service; perhaps these power struggles and opinions between the religious Clergy and Celebrants will fizz away, some day. Celebrants represent humanities best interest at heart; they have made a significant impact in places where only through Clergy could express and creatively forbidden were the rest. Funeral Celebrants are providing a service through a creative channel to express one's grief and giving the choice back to the public. In this way the family of the deceased can have a Celebrant and a religious figure of their choice to take part in the Ceremony? Empowering humanity with choice does not intend that the focus will be lost its meaning ? The Funeral Ceremony is to recognize and pay tribute to the life of the deceased. You are the Officiant, maintain this professionalism with the mourners; be courteous always and respectful of them, as well for the deceased. Do not be frightened of the Clergy it is a great opportunity and for those attending to experience.

The Funeral Officiant & Ceremony

Pricing Samples:

PACKAGE (A): STANDARD
PLANNING, PRACTICE, PERFORM–
. INITIAL INTERVIEW(OPTIONAL/SKYPE).
. Draft Ceremony
. Venue Liaison/visit (optional & varies)
. Draft Order of Ceremony
. Agree order of Ceremony and modify Draft
. Final Draft ~ To officiate with Ceremony for a 20 minute speaking.

PACKAGE (B): THE COMMITTAL/BENEDICTION
The initial 25% payment is § 31. 25
. A 2-8 MINUTE CLOSING OFF CEREMONIAL SPEAKING --------------- $ 125.00
CUSTOMARILY A VERY IMPORTANT PART OF THE CEREMONY IS TO CLOSE OFF WITH A FEW LAST WORDS AND THAT FURTHER INFORMATION IS WELL IMPARTED FOR AFTER EVENTS.
IN LIEU OF SUCH OCCASION THIS CAN BE WITH PACKAGE (H): A LA CARTE AS A CLOSING OFF POEM OR EXCERPT THAT CAN BE FIT TO AND CUSTOMIZE YOUR NEEDS.

MADE PERFECT FOR SEMI/SECULAR MEMORIAL TRIBUTES AND FOR SUCH OCCAISIONS AS WITH THE SCATTERING OF CREMATED REMAINS.

PACKAGE (C): BUDGET
. A 10-15 MINUTE CEREMONY ---

A VERY BRIEF/SHORT OFFICIATING/SPEAKING

PACKAGE (D): GRAVESIDE~ UNLESS ELABORATE AND SIMILAR TO A BUDGET CEREMONY
. A 15-20 MINUTE CEREMONY -----

AGAIN SIMILAR TO THE COMMITTAL SERVICE, IN THAT IT DOES NOT HAVE TO TAKE PLACE AT A CEMETERY, HOWEVER IS SOMEWHAT A LONGER SERVICE.

As the consumer can know what to expect; the more simple price list and packages can be explored and with much little, to none disappointments. Worth doesn't always identify itself to represent as the ideal poster boy or girl to hinge from image. Rather it is best represented by its depth in work and character, when given the opportunity. Most importantly a sense of clarity from doubt, is this level of transparency and to help build trust; eventually the less complicated everything will seem.

"BESPOKE YOUR CEREMONY"

PRICE LIST

PACKAGE (E): ELABORATE
The initial 25% payment is $175

STARTING FROM 40 MINUTES OF CEREMONY----------$700.00

~ A TRADITIONAL FUNERAL SERVICE DEPENDING ON THE RELIGION WITHIN A FUNERAL HOME CHAPEL AND/OR CHURCH CAN RUN FROM 30 MINUTES TO WELL OVER 2 HOURS. THIS PACKAGE CAN ALSO INCLUDE A COLLABORATIVE SEMI-SECULAR CEREMONY AND/OR A SECULAR FROM:

A FULL TRANSCRIPT; EVEN EULOGY WHEN THE MOURNER(S) WISH(E'S) TO BE THE MAIN SPEAKER(S) AND THEN SUMMARIZE TO ENSURE ALL THE REQUESTED INFORMATION IS IMPARTED.

PEERLESS MOMENTS COMES FROM A METAPHYSICAL PERSPECTIVE AND AS A NON DENOMINATIONAL SUPPORTER FOR ALL FAITHS !
WHETHER IT BE SEMI-SECULAR AND/OR RELIGIOUS;
THE LENGTH OF THE CEREMONY IS ENTIRELY UP TO THE TYPE OF SERVICE. FOR A SECULAR CEREMONY NORMALLY IS 40 MINUTES: WITH MUSIC; SPEAKERS; PERSONAL VIDEO MONTAGES AND LIKELY TO EXCEED LONGER WHEN THERE ARE MANY SPEAKERS.

ELABORATE CEREMONIES DEPEND ENTIRELY ON HOW EXPANSIVE THE DESIRE TO FULLY EXPRESS AND THE NEEDS OF THE MOURNERS GRIEF PROCESS !
~ ANYTHING GOES! The initial 25% payment is $250
THESE SERVICES CAN ADD UP TO AND RANGE IN FROM ---------- $ 1000.00

FOR EXAMPLE: A PRE-CEREMONY CAN TAKE PLACE DURING A 2 - 3 DAY SERVICE. WITH A FUNERAL PACKAGE THAT HAS VISITATIONS ON THE DAY BEFORE THE SERVICE; THE 40MINUTE CEREMONY ON THE DAY OF: CAN BE BROKEN DOWN AND OR FURTHER EXPANDED TO INCLUDE THESE SERVICES. SIMILAR TO THE COMMITTAL/BENEDICTION ON PACKAGE B TO CONSIDER, AND/OR PACKAGES C AND D; FROM WHICH THESE PRICES CAN BETTER REFLECT THE LENGTH OF SERVICES OFFERED. OTHER COSTS TO BE AGREED UPON PRIOR TO CEREMONY; MIGHT BE TO ADD SOME ELEMENTAL PROPS SUCH AS:

*THE BEATING OF A TRIANGLE BELL AS CUE FOR MOMENT OF SILENCE AND/OR WITHIN THE CEREMONY CAN BE PROVIDED

. THE LIGHTING OF CANDLES AND COLOURED SAND BOX

. WHITE DOVE RELEASE ~

. BALLOONS RELEASE ~ ---------- FROM $50.00

. TRAVEL EXPENSES ~ $2/KM IF OVER 30 KM TO VENUE/CLIENT.

The Funeral Officiant & Ceremony

What will your Slogan say and Branding look like ?

Peerless Moments
"BESPOKE YOUR CEREMONY"

PRICE LIST

PACKAGE (F): PRE-ARRANGED

The initial 25% payment is $93.75

UN OFFICIATED STANDARD CEREMONY PACKAGE ------------------------------ $375.00

~ ALTHOUGH A CONTRACT WITH EVERY PACKAGE IS PROVIDED; NOTHING HOWEVER WILL BE HELD IN TRUST AS AN INVESTMENT WITH A FINANCIAL INSTITUTION. YOU WILL ALWAYS GET WHAT YOU PAY FOR AND WITH PER EVERY AGREED UPON CONTRACT TO BE PROVIDED WITHIN A REASONABLE REFERENCE TIME PERIOD.

THIS WILL INCLUDE: A WRITTEN CEREMONY, MEMORIAL TRIBUTES, COMMEMORATIONS; OR ANY OTHER CONVENTIONALLY ACCEPTED AS DEALING WITH DEATH & LOSS.

A FILE IS CREATED ON RECORD FOR UP TO 10 YEARS AND ALSO A COPY GIVEN TO YOU OF THE FINAL DRAFT TO OFFICIATE WHENEVER AND BY WHOMEVER YOU PREFER!

ON THE DAY THIS EVENT IS TO TAKE PLACE AND/OR FEW DAYS PRIOR TO

PACKAGE (G): OFFICIATE THE PRE-ARRANGED STANDARD CEREMONY PACKAGE

The initial 25% payment is $43.75

OF CEREMONY FINAL DRAFT -------------------------------- $ 175.00
~TO OFFICIATE AND/OR MAYBE REVISE AN ALREADY PRE-EXISTING ORDER

PACKAGE (H): A LA CARTE ----------------------------

~ COMMEMORATIONS/MEMORIALS TRIBUTES/ AND/OR THE SCATTERING OF CREMATED REMAINS ARE SPECIAL EXTENSIONS OF WHICH TAKE PLACE AT A LATER TIME AND PLACE.

NOTE: 25% NON-REFUNDABLE DEPOSIT PAYABLE IN PERSON OR ONLINE BEFORE STARTING. FINAL AGREED INVOICE TO BE PAID IN FULL ON COMPLETION AND BEFORE THE CEREMONY IS TO TAKE PLACE.

You might want to keep it simple with only two umbrella type terms: "Celebration of Life" and/or "Memorials"; and/or ad an "Elaborate/Bespoke" Ceremony as a third umbrella option. The Following is a Pet Ceremony package and starting from with one starting price setting:

"BESPOKE YOUR CEREMONY"

PRICE LIST

PET MEMORIAL & TRIBUTE PACKAGE
PLANNING, PRACTICE, PERFORM---------------
OFFICIATING/SPEAKING. STARTING FROM ---------- $ 350.00

The Initial 50% payment is **$175**

- Ceremony Official package
- Unlimited telephone meetings and online consultations
- Draft Order of Ceremony
- Venue Liaison/visit (optional & varies)
- Agree Order of Ceremony & Modify
- Final Draft
- Officiate Ceremony (This is a 15min. service.... So Remember, anything beyond the 20min. leniency, will escalate the price range of package !)

- NB: 50% Initial Deposit Fee is Payable (IN PERSON OR ONLINE) before starting and with a 30% Non- Refundable.
- FINAL AGREED INVOICE/RECEIPT TO BE PAID IN FULL AND BEFORE THE CEREMONY IS TO TAKE PLACE.

. TRAVEL EXPENSES ~
Anything over a 30km range is subject to an additional $2/km consideration.

© 2019 Canadian Society of Celebrants   1

The Funeral Officiant & Ceremony

The Celebrant's Role:

Sometimes it may appear a bit redundant; however like with everything else, there is a reason for it. The initial meeting with the bereaved is the most crucial aspect of the Funeral Celebrant's role. This meeting allows you to share in the family's grief and suffering, especially when a death involves suicide, tragic accidents and children. Be harmonized with your roles when interviewing the bereaved; Grief Counselor (sensitively comfort listen and empathize) Information Gatherer/ Confident Organizer Guide.
The bereaved may be experiencing extreme all be it natural emotions and are likely to be unfamiliar with arranging Funerals. Your job is too literally or metaphorically, to set the scene and take them by the hand and guide / lead them through the process.
This process must be as pleasant as practicable, helpful but most importantly you must be sincere.

Making Initial Contact:

When making initial contact with the bereaved to organize a first meeting you must: Introduce yourself and briefly explain your role; pass on your condolences; motivate them to invite as many family and friends as possible to the meeting (brings depth and reality to your eulogy/ceremony). Encourage a home meeting; because the bereaved will feel more comfortable and open there.
Be flexible but firm and allow everyone to have an input.
Be adaptable but never judge; because every death has had own circumstances, and these situations the bereaved find themselves, in are also uniquely different. This is a bereavement process that will take time to reflect and heal. Invite the bereaved into this natural process of grief and through the important element of conversation about the deceased.

Go deeper with compassion :

After pleasantries are exchanged, it can be helpful to move away from small talk with compassion. Get a feel of your surroundings and the rhythmic flow of the bereaved in how they wish to express their view or any other topic that comes easily. When children are present, ask them their names or take the time to admire a baby when the feeling is there; that's how easy ice- breakers can be and watch the bereaved start feeling more at ease. The "elephant in the room" is most often the deceased, so this must be addressed as breaking the ice moment. The following sample can be easily adapted ... "*I did not know Jack/Jill; however it is important while I am here, to get a sense of who he/she was....I will be asking from you about their life and this may be upsetting for you; these questions might even be helpful to deal with what has happened. Is that ok?*" .... *Can you fill me in from your understanding; as to what happened that lead up to Jack's/Jill's death/passing?*" Gathering Information in this way and from what you have been provided from the "interview checklist"; It is a tool to help gather the information you are likely to need and for the experience.

Do not feel locked in to a strict order of questions; rather let the interview flow naturally. Be flexible and record answers and anecdotes as they are offered; whilst being careful to ensure all your questions are answered. It may also be helpful to indicate who said what, as this can be highlighted in the Ceremony itself. When the interview might feel strained; digress and talk about hobbies and interests of the deceased. The information can start to get overwhelming with many things thrown at you all at once from everywhere. Alternatively, ask questions that will help them focus on the bereaved that refer to fond memories or anecdotes and you will find that the atmosphere tends to become more uplifting as well as providing you with more valuable information.

The Funeral Officiant & Ceremony

Go deeper with compassion:

It is not uncommon for the bereaved to only mention the deceased's virtues and achievements and even exaggerate them which is fine. Listen with compassion when unkind human fragilities and failings surface, and be discerning with the Funeral Script, unless there is a humorous anecdote that accompanies and that the bereaved wish to be included. Aim to assemble a solid background understanding of the deceased through the interview, even when you do not use all the information. End the meeting with some business cards and where to be reached when something else might come to mind; to "send me an email as to add anything" Always leave the bereaved with some compassionate words.
It is a good feeling to leave knowing that they have confidence in you to conduct a memorable and meaningful Ceremony for the deceased.

Offering Ceremony Suggestions:

Think of a cover letter to a resume and how your packages explain your price list; the "Ceremony Suggestions" will further expand on what it is that you can offer. It was mentioned before of the "Interview Checklist" and "Questionnaire Sheet". Sometimes the questionnaire sheet is not enough of a pre ice breaker.
The bereaved might be too overcome with grief or not ready to discuss the life of the deceased. Another alternative to consider in their own time, might be; to email and/or to drop off your price list and packages you offer; along with the Interview Checklist and some suggestions in person. Is it appropriate to play music before the commencement of the Funeral Ceremony? This might be tranquil Funeral background music or your own choice.
Maybe they are interested in a Graveside Ceremony where, a portable music player can be used. Spoken Tributes from loved ones are wonderful, but, they may not be so easy to deliver.

Offering Ceremony Suggestions:

It is a good idea to write or type up speeches or readings so that in the event of a speaker faltering, the Celebrant can take over until the speaker has regained composure.

Sometimes participants in tandem can support each other. This is a good idea with children or teenagers.

Whether or not this is a religious Ceremony, it might be easier for loved ones to express themselves with such reading excerpts from the bible. An appropriate prayer can make great impact; the family and all those who are wishing to participate must specify what prayers should be included.

The Funeral Celebrant will then be able to officiate by introducing those who wish to, join in saying a prayer.

Suggest the option of a silent reflection time in the Ceremony. During this time music be played or an appropriate reading made. There can be time given for family members and loved ones, to come forward with their own tribute.

Photos and special memorabilia can be made for a great décor and/or theme for the service. A stand can be provided by the Funeral Director and set up in the foyer and/or a table can be placed at the front of the chapel to represent a life's journey.

An announcement about refreshments can be made at the Ceremony to give everyone somewhere to meet up afterward.

Setting Service Elements in Order:

Determine how the word will get out; for example: Is the "Celebration of Life" being held in conjunction with a traditional Funeral or Memorial service? These details can also be included in the death notice and/or obituary; as well as on social media. Is the a Celebration separate from a more traditional service and that is also to take place? Is the Celebrant Ceremony a stand alone; or will it take place sometime in the future? Invitations are not normally sent for Funerals; Perhaps an added step of calling or writing a note to those who may not be active online?

Memorials:

Allotting the opportunity for friends and family to gather from further afield and to create a greater scope to include the memories of others. Together with the Celebrant a truly personal and bespoke "Celebration of Life" can take place. Reflections on a life lived well After the Funeral Service. A service provided for the deceased and without their physical body present. It can be a "Tribute" of the life and achievements and their associations that your loved one had. By organizing a Memorial, you are afforded the leisure to gather stories and anecdotes; a particular skill that can be showcased and proper respect paid to their interests and that perhaps was missed before. When "Summing Up" with the bereaved during the Ceremony; always acknowledge to give them thanks after the speakers have completed their Tributes. Give them this public recognition; that they have performed well on all the great number of readings and eulogies Celebrating the deceased.

Reflection Time:

Rather than focusing on a group intention unlike praying; reflecting and releasing is more about creating a safe and supported space to grieve. It is just another way to incorporate and as mentioned before "A Moment of Silence". Just another name to cover over the idol thought of being religious in its content and can be perceivable as a form of meditation. Naturally appropriated for the use of prayer; allowances must be given for the bereaved and mourners and that matter in this way of practice. Rather a reflection time unlike the specified "Moment of Silence" will include a reading of an appropriate piece of prose or poetry. Again a Moment Of Silence and as explained before; it is simply a snippet moment taken to reflect(30seconds to2 minutes).

Reflection Time:

"Reflection Time" can also take place while music is played if required; perhaps the bereaved might want to sing along or in their thoughts or silent prayer be added. Attention may also be drawn, during the reflection time, to a photograph; a slideshow; and/or personal memorabilia, to help focus on. Ideas for an appropriate reflection time can be discussed with the bereaved at the initial interview. The time to reflect can also take place while waiting for the Ceremony to take place and/or after sociably around refreshments. It has become customary for refreshments to be made available after the Funeral Ceremony, allowing the family of the deceased and friends to gather in a less formal environment and comfort each other, swap stories and share memories. Ideally, after discussing with the bereaved, you will be able to announce it in your introductory remarks or at the very end that refreshments will be available(where/Venue/when) after the Ceremony's conclusion.

Order of Ceremony:

Whether or not to have a printed Order of Ceremony is a personal choice of the bereaved. To many it is a Memorial and record of this occasion applicable to the deceased. It can list what songs are to be sung and even the lyrics to sing along with. An Order of Ceremony is necessary so that people can follow the words and join in. Most of the time it is added in with the Funeral service's package and the Funeral establishment does print them out. Generally, the Order of Ceremony is kept simple and comprised of a two-page(A4) document. Other designs, such as bookmarks and greeting card sized documents are becoming more popular.

Simple Sample: Order of Service for a Funeral and Memorial
Prelude->Welcome Opening Prayer Hymn/Song Scriptures of Comfort and Hope; Eulogies, Poem, Meditation and Closing Prayer Postlude *******

The Funeral Officiant & Ceremony

Order of Ceremony:

The Celebrant could cater to providing a public leaflet or manual of the order of service. In this case it is considered in with packages and added in the price list; as a courtesy create a few samples to showcase for the bereaved. Before agreeing to do this for the bereaved; always consult with all parties involved and so that it does not overlap, with any other provider's services.
As mentioned in the example(A4): a standard sheet of paper with both sides utilized and folded in half. A vertical $8^{1/2}$ cover that opens from right to left. On the cover can be written the name of the venue (where it is to take place); the type of Ceremony service to be held and when(dateAndTime). Inside the left side can be an opening reading and/or verse to describe the theme(ritual element); for example a "Candlelight Vigil" might have the entire page be printed candles on a coloured photo and on the candle the opening reading. To the right on the next fold of the page will be the "Order of Service" and on the back closing of the cover side a closing statement giving thanks from the organizers with their printed logo and branding of business. Make it festive looking and appealing to the viewer. The following outline was designed by the establishment; it did not have a proper Officiant set in place.
The venue staff preferred this option and unknowingly had blended; from what appeared to be (the making of) an "Anatomy of Ceremony" and along with the "Order of the Ceremony".
This is how we learn sometimes and on who decides these rules is not so important as is the authenticity. Who decides what; is this collaborative co-creation of trusted connections and a healthy integration of these contacts. The one taking on the Celebrant's role perhaps had no idea and this is why he was the chosen of the bunch. This was progress in the making and while others in the back ground sat and watched(listened to the Funeral staff perform).

Order of Ceremony:

Taken into consideration; the following creation was exquisite and in blending the responsibilities(of roughly who does what). The book can show, to sample its idea; however it cannot give the recognition and feeling of entitlement to those inspired agendas. It can only show with good intentions what the driving force created and not the origin of program.

Order of Service

Prelude.......

Welcome and greetings(Officiant)

Introduction......(Celebrant)

Candle Lighting(The Venue responsible for making these leaflets)

Reflection...(Celebrant)

Musical Selection...(Male vocalist on guitar)

Poetry Reading(Funeral Director's Daughter)

Memorial Slide Show Tribute

Blessing and Tribute..(Celebrant)

Postlude.......

We all know how to make examples of ourselves and other people; however do we know exactly how to set the proper standards? The answer is, through the same way as the above establishment had for many years; the space and patrons from which to practice on. It is through this kind of role modeling and in the act of freely giving, for those who can; to willingly do so and from their kindness of their heart. It is from this karmic ripple that we want, of accepting to receive and give.
That is what makes any act of kindness so special....

Gratitude for the space we hold and appreciation of our service !

The Funeral Officiant & Ceremony

Order of Ceremony:

The following is a basic outline of an actual Order of Ceremony; (as witnessed with the previous Memorial grouping) in this case it is for a Funeral service Ceremony, more of these can be sampled; however the reader must learn(with your own version)to recreate and best adapt for their own purposes.

Outline Funeral Order of Ceremony (suggestions only, all optional).

Music Playing on Entry(Organ, or CD/USB)

Opening Remarks (to introduce the occasion)

Introductory Sentences

All Sing or Say a Verse(To help us to gather)

One or more Readings (Expressing the beliefs of those assembled regarding life, death and mourning)

Eulogy: Describe in a tribute or appreciation for the life of the departed(Said by a member of the family or by the Celebrant)

Music or Quiet – Moment of Silence to reflect

Words of Comfort, Encouragement (e.g. "To all the [so and so] who I loved before and those who loved me back")

Concluding with a verse said all together(some request the Lord's Prayer)

All Sing or Say a Verse (To strengthen us for the moment of parting)

Words of Committal (perhaps music played as curtains close)

Closing Words Close - Music played (Giving time for everyone to compose themselves before leaving).

Order of Ceremony:

One might think the Order of a Ceremony as meaningless and harmless; rather next to the Anatomy of Ceremony it sets the platform and ambiance. These particulars are essential insights to be gained and by the certain order, an atmosphere of expectation. To conclude the following such said and that can begin from: An Opening Reading->An opening verse-> Depending on the personality of the deceased and the wishes of the bereaved; it may be appropriate theme(light hearted, tragic….) thoughts on Life & Death of the deceased and all the many others that they/we are grieving for.

The importance of: The Anatomy of A Ceremony !

The Anatomy is similar to the "Order of Service".
It is a walk through the entire Ceremony; however much like a rehearsal. Just like any other special event a plan must be set in place. It allows us to officiate even for the unexpected and unscripted details to take place; these interactions of the flow and rhythm heartfelt moments. Although improvising without a script is not a good recommendation, this is how it can be slotted in. The Anatomy of A Ceremony is the key element for whom so ever wishes to conduct the Ceremony.
While the Order of Ceremony is created for the Bereaved to follow along; the Anatomy Of Ceremony is exclusively designed to walk the Celebrant through each and every step, of who is doing what and when. In many instances and when dealing with other kind of Ceremonies; a walk through is more private, less formal and highly recommended.
When confronted with a loss it becomes a healing journey through grief. The Anatomy Of A Ceremony allows for a co-creative palette and much collaboration to take place.

The Funeral Officiant & Ceremony

The importance of: The Anatomy of A Ceremony !

It is wise to ask each wishing participant to write down exactly what is desired at a Memorial. These directives can include friends and other mourners of their circle. Not only in Memorials; but also when the deceased is present and for all the services included. Choice of music, pallbearers, Clergy, interment, and any other details. With the decedent's directives taken into consideration, the family must be consulted of their wishes and outweigh the traditions of any. It is vital that all options for honoring the loved one be presented; they need to know not only what should be done(according to tradition), or what has always been done; but also what can be done, to memorialize their loved one. It would be a sad situation for the family to learn, after the service, what they could have had, but it wasn't part of this tradition. The family can select only those elements of the service they wish to have included and can decline as being too traumatic. Again, survivors must be taken through the options presented; but not be pressured into including any tradition. Cross-cultural Funeral services are perhaps a bit more stylish and might reflect on the Secular types of Ceremony; rather than the ancestral and shift toward contemporary.
Many sub-cultural and more unique traits can be observed from these kind of Semi-Secular events and venues. For example, a Nigerian Funeral might be steeped in ritual and more persistently traditional. The burial amongst them might be highly ritualized, with deep mourning and very serious; several months later, they might want to hold a second Graveside service, accompanied by feasting and merry making. This is where a "Celebration of Life" Ceremony can come in real handy. Then from the West, the Caribbean hold many Elaborate Ceremonies; from Protestant to Baptist and a wide array of burial, as well as cremation.

The importance of: The Anatomy of A Ceremony !

The changes toward a Semi-Secular component has been well received; in that the order of service to include is far more Secular in its collaborations. Services are held in Funeral homes mostly than they are in churches, and the music is more contemporary, like jazz playing in the background.

The higher the social positioning of the deceased the more elaborate it can become in its complexity. With Semi-Secular, a lot can go wrong especially, without any traditional guidelines of co-operation and with a priesthood that speaks in many tongues. The gender here is very closed and as it would be, with many other religions; such as, Muslim and Judeo-Christian Values. What the Celebrant can do in these cases, is to take this providence of importance and make relevant to independently Officiate for any and/or all the segments that it might impact to serve with a scripted Ceremony and be it performed with grace. Just what are we looking at here?

The actual approach to the funeral event will vary depending on the particular community. For some, the Funeral is a joyous celebration, for others the event is more solemn. Eulogies often focus on family and faith. Spiritual music is customary and may include contemporary religious selections as well as hymns. A viewing is customary and may include commemoration of the deceased secular activities such as participation in community or fraternal organizations. Normally a Baptist Ceremony(King James Bible) can go up to an hour however sometimes as in the case below there could be made exceptions. Unlike many other denominations this example could be best fitting; as there are no formal rules to becoming ordained. A Pastor can easily be replaced with a Celebrant Officiant; likewise the Pastor can take the Bishop's place to work alongside with the Celebrant.

The Funeral Officiant & Ceremony

The importance of: The Anatomy of A Ceremony !

Note from previously given Order of Service example(Candlelight Memorial); there are no rules on who must lead and who must follow and/or commence with intro; or who gives off the closing words. Just as long as the finances(if any), are well negotiated ahead of time. In most cases it is left up to the family and preference of its congregation; also the religious(bible of choice) aspects are better serviced by the Pastor and/or Bishop.
More about Scripture readings Vs. Excerpts reads and/or poems will be explored later through this book. The following will be a filled out skeletal template to sample; from a Baptist Ceremony and that can be turned into a Semi-Secular celebration. In this way the Ceremony service can be focused on the spiritual elements, as well as the religious facets. So what we will then end up having is a service that can go on from the normal half-hour to an hour.
The venue in the following scenario was booked for 3 hours and the Ceremony service was to last from 10 a.m. to 11:30 a.m.
The participants, regardless of the amount scripted (handed over to the Celebrant to add in script) had to be given limits of 5 minutes each; as not all had given; nor completed what they wanted to say, until that very moment (they were to speak publicly).
Do not worry so much about the timing here, as it will become more important in the Script. The actual timing for the entire Ceremony will be all mapped out within the making of the Ceremony Draft and not in the Anatomy of the Ceremony so much so not to be concerned about.

In this case scenario the Celebrant was paid handsomely; had ample(21days) time and a semi-rehearsal; with mostly all participants present.

ACIFC   CSOC

Contact: _____ **WIFE** _____ Ceremony Type: **FUN**/WED/ROV/NAM
Client(s): __Wendelin Mason Cavalier__ Venue: __Anytime F.H.C.__ Date: _25/ 10 / 2019._

START

Officiate's Responsibilities	Responsibility of Others
Meet & Greet	FD Preps with chapel/casket/usb
Cue Processional Music (20min)	Video Tribute ~Instrumental Worship
	Choir & staging crew gathers/ all systems in place
Cue walk-in(side by side) with Minister (left side) followed by Funeral Staff. I veer off to the right side of chancel.	Precious Lord Take My Hand Song F.D. leads the way. Instrumental~Staff Close Casket/Exit
PBS–Welcome Introduction/who you are Remembrance~ **at 55 Kendall Cavalier, a.k.a. Doeg,** 1963-2019 (day of memories)	
Admin(asking to switch off all gadgets & sitdown) after ceremony where to go if charitable collection on departure.	
Introduce the Speaker	
Words on Grief (Job 19:25/KJV)	The Bishop takes over with scripture John 11:11 and 14:2/ Romans 8:37/39
Scene I: Come in and moderate	All rise
Describe what he was like And start to build his portrait (5min.)	
Introduce the Chorister Praise & Worship (6min.)	Chorister takes centre stage/intro; Asks everyone seated to stand&join in. Choir gets up and starts singing.
Scene II: Come in and preside	Everyone takes their seat back down.
Reader 1 (John 11:14-25)	Doeg's Sister(comes forward)Reads
Left side face & enter on stage again. Introduce~Nephew(BeulahLand)to sing.	Doeg's Nephew(given 5min.)shares a few words. Reads Poem&Sings Tribute Song.
Scene III: Come in and finish describing (KC's portrait). (10min.)	
Eulogy 1	Work affiliate/Best friend-Tribute
Give Thanks and introduce next	
Eulogy 2~Reflection of Life	Another pastor gives a Tribute (20min.)
Reflection-Song by Choir	Everyone starts singing
Scene IV: Please be seated/ Reader 2	Daughter reads a scripture
Give thanks/introduce – poem reader.	Niece reads poem.
Close it off	Choir and Bishop take over

FINISH

The Funeral Officiant & Ceremony

The importance of: The Anatomy of A Ceremony !

Most of the time a Funeral Ceremony and only on the very rarest of occasion; might it take the opportunity for somewhat of a rehearsal. This is why these structured templates are so important and even better when applied to such cooperation of rehearsal.
Knowing the right protocol and Order of the Ceremony can also be very valuable in cases such as the planning of Firefighter and Law Enforcement Funeral service rituals and Memorials.
More will be discussed on these types of venues and what to expect so when asked you will know exactly how you can fit yourself in and where you will be valued. They are the most challenging given the opportunity to adapt with such customs that are steeped in Tradition but not necessarily religious. The following samples are merely that. They serve to provide an appropriate skeleton of a Funeral Ceremony on which to build on and adapt to your style.

After being given a few samples on the various "Order of Services" and how to create the skeletal Anatomy of Ceremony application. The following is from a Memorial service Ceremony program and that was then put together into a booklet format; for everyone to follow along during the event. See how you can find it useful with the Anatomy Of Ceremony Application.

You are asked to officiate collaboratively to create this Ceremony and come up with a program. Can you recreate it into the Anatomy Of Ceremony Model?

(Lest We Forget)Remembrance Day Order of (100ᵗʰ Commemorative)Ceremony:

- To the right of the Cenotaph reserved seating is provided(Veterans, Royal Canadian Legion).

- The public congregates at Toronto's Old City Hall Cenotaph(1914-1918)&(1950-1953)

- Introduction(Officiating Speaker to the podium>Chaplain of Toronto Fire Fighter services)

- Members of the official party and replaying party(all other military configurations of parade and marching contingents); that will shortly join in(with flags in linear stance to stand on middle platform of the stairs and along each side of the podium),to make their way out from the entrance of Old City Hall. Marching Soldiers(Toronto Civic Honour guards and Uniform services) as their representing officials(RCL/Armed Forces) to take their place around the Cenotaph and in preparation for that Moment of Silence.

- The Officiate Speaker (in recognition of all Chippewa treaty bands and the traditional aboriginal territory; as well as the many nations of Inuit and Metis people) On behalf for all that are present for this Ceremony. Then speaker will ask "all to stand who can"; until "The Act of Remembrance" and "Commitment to Remember" is read.

- National Anthem(all rise and join in the singing)
- Last Post
- Two Minute of Silence
- Lament(passionate expression of grief)

The Funeral Officiant & Ceremony

(Lest We Forget)Remembrance Day Order of (100th Commemorative)Ceremony:

- Rouse(bring out of sleep)

- Canadian Harvard Aircraft Association "Fly-By"

- "Act of Remembrance" reading(D-Day Veteran)

- Commitment to Remember(Oji-Cree) Reading(RisingAboveMinistry/Aboriginal Pastor)

- Commitment of Remember(French) Reading(Grade 9-blond girl/Catholic student)

- Address the gathering to worship(City[5min.]Mayor)and welcoming in the support

- "O God, Our Help In Ages Past"~R.C. Hymn(song)

- Officiating Speaker~To introduce next 2 speakers to read "In Flanders Fields"

- Leading Air Cadet and Master Seaman read poem~"In Flanders Fields"

- Officiating Speaker~("Poem was written by" and goes to further describing the history behind the symbol of the Poppy~then introduces next segment)

- Moment of Silence while Officiating Speaker/Chaplain (Fire Services) leads in Prayer(for the Fallen and those left behind to find their peace within forgiveness)

(Lest We Forget) Remembrance Day Order of (100th Commemorative) Ceremony:

- Wreath Laying~ "Hymn To Freedom" (during the laying down of wreaths) The representatives of governments; Armed Forces; Veterans and other such organized associations, start placing their wreaths (from level of importance down)

- Officiating speaker addresses them as they pick up the lined up wreathes from stand just below the stairs from the podium toward and in between the 2 soldiers that are standing back to back and place onto Cenotaph(CityMayor; The parliament and Government of Canada; MPP; Veteran's AffairRep.; RCNavy[commanders; lieutenants]; Canadian Brigade and Army; RCLegionDistrictD; Members of The Counselors of Corps; Old Comrades[36div.]Ass; Army/Navy/Air force; IrishV. Ass./Korean War Vets. Vietnamese;) (Maltese Ass.; Naval club; RCA; Military/Vimy; Police/Fire/Public Servants and so on).

- Hymn To Freedom-Choir

- Benediction(Officiant's last words/a request blessing by Christ; then introduces "RA")

- Royal Anthem

- March Off

The Funeral Officiant & Ceremony
Chapter V

Tragic Deaths:

Funerals can be tragic affairs for the family and friends of the deceased, but never is this more so than when unexpected deaths occur and people are taken before their time, with so much to offer. A Funeral Ceremony for someone that has died tragically should concentrate on the part of the decedent's life that can be celebrated and shared rather than the manner of their passing.

Ceremony for a Victim of Murder

Like the loss of life for suicide, how can one express, soften or even address the feeling of a bereaved family when a life is lost through murder? The service may be almost like a therapy session; it takes the utmost of care to approach, under such terrible circumstances. Family members overwhelmingly feel disbelief, numb and distrustful of life. The act of grieving might seem senseless; because it won't bring back their loved one. It can be extremely difficult to collect sufficient information for a meaningful eulogy; cast your information gathering net a little wider. As with suicides, emotions can be smitten and the bereaved are struggling with bitterness, rage and despair. Relatives and friends my be a little on the spiteful and making snide remarks. Difficulty in communicating and the ability to express of themselves is next to none. Ceremony for a young teenager is likely to have parental involvement and an even more highly charged emotional atmosphere. Look to cater for the possibility of coaching friends of the deceased; who are similarly aged and wish to pay tribute during the Ceremony. These Ceremonies are the most emotionally charged; potentially because, the mourners are in the same age bracket as the deceased and a little less mature of their emotions. With Ceremony for a "Suicide and/or Drug Related Death"; the feelings of the family will dictate the mood of the service.

Tragic Deaths:

Emotions can confuse decision making it can be difficult to disclose information. Many families choose not to make any reference to the nature of the death; while others prefer a more open and transparent method for this reference to be made.
As much as the bereaved do try to hold back, accept their struggle and that they will explode from time to time.
The cluster of emotion that grief does hold but to name a few as guilt, fear, anger, shame; well beyond those experienced in other types of death. So you must be especially patient, compassionate and understanding during your initial interview. The deceased in many cases could have suffered with bouts of depression over several years; it may help families to communicate this fact to other mourners. The more transparency that can be offered from family to friends; it can lift the mood somewhat.
The more united the mourners can be open and accepting, in this warmth of tears and love; the more uplifting rather than a somber mood. With the above said, create the Ceremony (as far as is possible) and walk into it with great reverence.

Ceremony for an Infant:

The death of a baby can be a challenge for a Funeral Celebrant; because the usual practice of focusing on a life lived, and the experiences shared of good times does not apply. We are faced with an opportunity to create a meaningful ritual; it will mark the loss of a life unlived, of good times never shared and of a life that was expected but cut short. You must be able to connect with the grieving parents and family; examine as best you can their expectations of the love that was shared with their baby and in preparing for his/her arrival. Yes, it is possible to mark the occasion and to prepare a service every bit as meaningful, even for a stillborn baby. Participating may help them to start the initial grieving process; by enabling them to channel their grief in to a meaningful activity rather than inwardly containing it. Encourage the parents to plan the Ceremony, selecting readings and verses.

The Funeral Officiant & Ceremony

Public Speaking and Officiating:

Speaking from the heart or off by heart is always best!
This will entail much practice and rehearsing; unless that which you have to say is most important to you in the first place. Sometimes there is a following established; at other times the magnetism must be found from unknown others and who can resonate for an attraction. At this point of contact, is where the soft spot for making the connection is with your audience. Give this gathering from that level of interest and go deeper into what they will find meaningful. The attraction is in the title; it will furthermore question its theme and by elaborating on the thesis statement. The thesis must hold magnetism to draw the audience deeper into subject matter. The narrative(s) add(s) relevance for the sharing of experience(s) and the value that it can hold with your audience. Then leave them with the many probabilities from which to wonder from their own perspective and off into expansion.
How many different perceptions can be given from these statement points? For all intensive purposes the Anatomy of Ceremony was given so that the student can learn how to officiate. On the other hand but not necessary as to suggest the speaker be your only role on stage; where a skeletal version of your presentation exclusively geared for going on stage would be as follows: Make from your pointers q-cards and/or pointers; they will be brief reminders of what you will be going further deeply into adlibbing experiences from the heart. The key pointers will help you to release you into inspiration and trigger from this place of passion; this way it will get others to want to engage and without getting off track.
The "Anatomy Of Ceremony" can do just that for your script to be officiated by you for this entire Ceremony and as it would the many other speakers on track. This is the importance of building a structure. With structure the Ceremony can flow in and with every step well guided into the event, including public speaking.

Public Speaking and Officiating:

Another important fundamental is rehearsal; because the timing must be well adjusted and just the same as speaking the anatomy as well for the entire ceremony of events.

The public speaking of the script is what you must practice on your own to know it well with confidence. Your heart will be racing and it might feel like popping out of your chest; do not mistaken this excitement with fear. You might want to try practicing in front of a mirror and or even film yourself and play it back. Learning how to become the observer in this case of yourself is the best way of establishing your mindfulness.

You will find your way and the more you practice; the more you will believe in the words coming out of your mouth and perhaps from memory(from heart). When with your presence you present unscripted; it is essential to have some kind of key points to reference from and be supported. Power points will give us the ability to stay on track and focused; draw from them rather than become distracted when your audience's unrelated thoughts to question from your statements and distort the intended agendas meaning. There is always going to be some kind of anatomical structure to help guide along the direction and that of the order for these focal points; as well as final execution for the agenda's entire motive of intention. Public speaking with a script requires rehearsing; as well as an anatomy of the order of events the script must follow to officiate. In other words the "Anatomy of The Ceremony" is essential for the purpose of "Officiating:

And not so much for public speaking. Rather to know when to come in and take your place and when to speak; these will be the order of events that are to take place as you officiate them for the Ceremony. The Anatomy will help you to synchronistically conduct and synergize the Ceremony and not so much as the script would have you publicly speak and present your content.

The Funeral Officiant & Ceremony

Officiants/Celebrants:

We have witnessed from previously reading and thus far that anything goes; just as long as we know our place. We can be Celebrants as well as Officiants and/or just Officiants; either/or, we must be paid for our services (ranging anywhere from $150-$300). As in this case, Funeral establishments can be our clients; as well as hold the venue and often will insist on the Officiating themselves exclusively; when (on their punch clock) they are the ones paying us (hourly) then by all means. There is no doubt of the strenuous work behind the scenes; that must take place with management and the Funeral staff of many helpers alike. The team grunt too, it is rewarded; but not always in the spot light gathering the praise for it. When the bereaved have hired us directly; then we will not be, as hired Funeral Directing staff or helpers to assist with the service. Make no mistake of your role and that you have been hired as an agent to carry out this Ceremony. It might take extra contracts as previously shown and in order for the Funeral staff to collaborate with us; because we are third party contractors and we must be clear about this role. Reconcile in cooperation, the diming of ones light over another's; are these incompatibilities and they make every one look sloppy.

https://www.youtube.com/watch?v=Uqs17_FaZW4&t=1s

This way everyone involved can be participating and respected for the role they do serve. Celebrants must be professional to work with families. We design a service that is customized to their cultural, religious, and spiritual needs. We can be trained to know when to be humble and when to stand up and be firm; to properly guide and assist in the arranging of both Secular and Non-Secular celebrations. Our services are not limited to Celebrations of Life. They often work with people planning a traditional Funeral or Memorial services as well. The Canadian Society Of Celebrants are qualified in this role of Officiants, as well as helping to plan the service.

Setting the Tone within the opening of the Ceremony:

The opening is arguably the most crucial part of a Funeral Ceremony as it sets the tone and pace of what is to follow. Gain the mourners trust and reassurance so they can feel and/or start to feel more at ease. From the very beginning is this captured moment for the grieving loved ones and to reconnect with the personality of the deceased. In the previous section we addressed the process of the Initial Interview. In the next step is this process of writing an opening to a Funeral Ceremony. What follows is merely a framework from which you can compose your own. From this sample make useful to customize for your own; the many variations and that will enable you to provide given your own imagination and bereaved involved.

Introducing Yourself

It is a matter of choice whether you introduce yourself formerly or not. In the previous case scenario: the Order of Ceremony, was very keen to mentioned its valued participants.
From that and any other Order of Ceremony that is accustomed to advertise in this way and in it negating the need to introduce yourself verbally to the mourners gathered. In any case,
do introduce yourselves as it is always best to make it clear and promote yourself in this way of given opportunity.
The simplest of introductions will suffice, for example:
  "Good Morning, and welcome to the Funeral Ceremony for ...." OR
  "My name is ...., I am a Funeral Celebrant and it is my privilege to be conducting this Ceremony for .... today"

Setting the Tone within the opening of the Ceremony:

An Opening Reading:

An opening verse is a great way to create a feeling of comfort and to set the tone for the service. Eventually the interest to invest your very own samples of poems and prose is awesome; however it is even better to actually make up your own. For all intensive purposes the safest way to start; is by utilizing "Unknown Authors" and the following is simple enough to grasp:

"IT HAS BEEN SAID THAT – LOVE DOES NOT END WITH DYING OR LEAVE IN THE LAST BREATH. FOR SOMEONE YOU HAVE LOVED DEEPLY, LOVE DOES NOT END WITH DEATH". Author Unknown

Another popular verse is:
"I ASK NOT WEALTH, NOR LENGTH OF DAYS NOR PRIDE NOR POWER, NOR WORLDLY PRAISE".
"PERHAPS, A LITTLE QUIET PLACE WHERE A FRIEND MAY COME AND OPEN THE DOOR AS THOUGH IT WERE HOME". Author Unknown

The more a Ceremony can be tailored to the individual who has died, the better. Practice with great interest in this kind of creativity. After so many collected number of readings and verses; it will become a straightforward task and to draw upon from your very own inspirational words. Keep it simple always and start from there, with the opening. This is how the space becomes created and allow for the mourners to make up for the rest. The bereaved will be able to contemplate amongst themselves and from their own thoughts; rather than digest a long complicated reading.

Setting the Tone within the opening of the Ceremony: Opening Verses for Tragic Circumstances !

Many Funeral Ceremonies are penetrated with extreme grief and sadness. The intoxicated grief from some deaths of young people, tragic accidents, and suicides. "Sometimes the lingering of such deep grief; it will allow for the exhibit of courage and strength": by asking of the mourners, "to unite and to help each other through their pain". The Strength of such a space is very much valued and to share as they go through this tragic loss of life. Along with by providing the strength and comfort in its time of need; another "Opening" to sample: *"WE GATHER TO HONOUR [First Names] MEMORY AND TO SUPPORT ONE ANOTHER IN GRIEVING THE DEATH THAT IS THE HARDEST DEATH TO GRIEVE: DEATH THAT WAS CHOSEN".* In this case of a suicide; going directly into the introduction is alright too. At this point there is obviously any number of different words you might use. There follows yet another; "OUR GRIEF AND *SORROW IS ALL THE MORE PAINFUL FOR THE PASSING OF THIS YOUNG SOUL* (or just replace it with the word) *"MAN". "THE LOSS OF SUCH A FINE YOUNG MAN IS RIGHT DOWN SHOCKING TO SAY THE LEAST". "IT IS UNLIKE THE DEATH OF AN ELDERLY FRIEND; IN THAT THEY LIVED ALL THEY COULD POSSIBLY STRETCH INTO THIS LIFE AND BE IT RECOGNIZED A NORMAL CHANGE THE END OF AWARENESS AND US IN THEM AND ALL THAT THEY HAVE ACHIEVED". THE LEGACY THEY COULD HAVE LEFT BEHIND; THE MOUNTAINS THEY HAD YET TO CLIMB AND OTHER CONQUESTS FAR AND WIDE".*

The Funeral Officiant & Ceremony

Setting the Tone within the opening of the Ceremony:

The Introduction:

Once you have completed your opening verse you will need to make some introductory remarks to simply outline the procedure and the purpose of the day's Ceremony.
Start off by identifying "all those who have gathered here today" and the family of _____ thank you, for coming to celebrate the life of(so and so)". "At times like this we are naturally enveloped in a melting pot of emotions; sorrow, sadness, grief not to forget the memories, happiness the purpose of a life well lived".
It is then worth explaining the procedure for after the Funeral; however (you might consider the time restraint) to leave it at the end for the Funeral Director to express. Often it is left up to the family to gathering up the mourners, at their home/local club or similar facility. A cup of tea and/or coffee can make for a comforting relief for many of the mourners; however it is not a mandatory consideration for the Funeral establishment to provide.
To go over it a few several times again; the "Introduction" following this sample to consider: *"I thank you all for being here today, as we commemorate with sorrow, respect, joy and thankfulness the life of [full name]". "At the end of this Ceremony you are all invited for some snacks and hot beverages at the [name the place], for a chat and to recollect the special times you spent with [full name]". "Death, in a number of ways, unites us all, for it demands that each of us put aside our own trials and tribulations to unite ourselves with everyone here gathered". This is a common thread that weaves the tapestry of our experiences we have shared to bond with love and respect for [first name]".* Obviously, the above will be tailored to the deceased.

Setting the Tone within the opening of the Ceremony:

The Introduction

The following is made to sample of an elderly deceased person:

I am sure that [first name] would not want you to grieve in hurt or pain, but grieve in the joy that she has given, that she has received and that she has shared. And so it is thinking of [first name] and saying goodbye and we can say thank you to [first name] and celebrate a life well lived. For a young deceased person the following can be said; "*When we lose someone so young and dear to us, the hurt can seem unbearable. Yet the hurt inside gives us strange comfort, as it tells us just how much we loved them. As we reminisce our dearly beloved [first name] today and for what he/she has given us; that we can say thank you [first name] and goodbye*". In many cases, a family member or friend will present a tribute or reading, but the Celebrant will be left to present the actual eulogy. At other times, a good friend or relative will present the eulogy in whole. It may be that you are asked to take care of all the readings, or at least prepare the readings for the bereaved to read. These options should be discussed with the bereaved at the Initial Interview.

We have already gone through how to go about preparing the heart of the Ceremony, but for the sake of leaving anything out, and including readings that can be to recommend to the family when they might not be sure what they like. When a Celebrant gets asked to officiate at a Funeral Ceremony; it indicates that the bereaved are not adhering to any specific church or religion. After the opening reading and/or verse, is the introduction and as mentioned in chapter II; preparing for the eulogy is this chronological next step.

The Funeral Officiant & Ceremony

Preparing the Eulogy:

To sum up; take ownership of the Eulogy and prepare it as though there will be no other speakers at the Ceremony. Regardless of whether there are several relatives or friends of the deceased giving tributes, it is wise to be prepared in the event of anyone faltering. Other contributors may not have included something that the Celebrant could have recorded during the initial interview; perhaps light-hearted, and/or maybe important or even something trivial. Also, to sum up at the conclusion of the Ceremony, some extra tidbits can be added; to widen the perspective of the tribute being paid to the deceased. Always be prepared and have a copy of what contributors intend to say. The introduction for the eulogy was already suggested with a few samples before; however the following simple introduction may be appropriate: *In the next few minutes it is my privilege to share with you the life of [full name] As well as sharing in his/her life, we also share in our grief for his/her death. After speaking with the family, I know that they would not want you to grieve in hurt or pain but grieve in the joy that [first name] has given, has received and has shared with each of you here today".*
Introduce the Eulogies by family and friends and keep it simple; *"As a tribute to [first name], her/his daughter, Jane will now share her thoughts with us. Jane, please come forward".*
Remember to ensure that the names of family and friends are accurately recorded and spelled out phonetically; it is necessary to facilitate properly pronounced introductions.

Tributes & Readings:

As previously mentioned, it may be beneficial for the Celebrant to carry a collection of sample readings and tributes for the bereaved (to gain inspiration from) during the Initial Interview. Adapt and/or adopt for the bereaved to choose for their particular service. The Ceremony can often have more of an impact, when two or more of the bereaved take part delivering elements of the same tribute or reading. The following is an excerpt sample of a Tribute to a Father and Grandfather:

" So loving and kind was our father; a wonderful grand dad, brother and husband. What beautiful memories [Benjamin] does leave behind with us and many to share amongst us. He was indeed a very caring and sharing and always content gentleman, loved and respected wherever he went. Benjamin left with us his happy smile, a heart of gold and in our hearts, he was the best this world could hold. What beautiful memories we all have of you".
~Nohah

Summing Up:

When the bereaved have taken the opportunity to perform speaking; have completed their part of the readings and eulogies of the deceased, thank them all and sum up. The following is an excerpt sample for a Final Tribute and of a Ceremony for a victim of suicide(keep it short and pause enough for meaning).

The Funeral Officiant & Ceremony

Summing Up:

From the Ceremony of a Suicide Final Tribute (kept short and sweet):

You tried so hard you told so few
We will never know what you went through

You never failed to do your best
Your heart was true and tender
You simply lived for those you loved
And those you loved – will remember

Readings Prior to Committal:

Many Funeral Celebrants move seamlessly from the eulogies and readings to the Committal, however, you may wish to attempt to soften the impact of the Committal with:
When someone we love dies, we are faced with trying to understand life's final journey. The following words may give you a way of looking at death that is comforting, and that makes it just a little easier to come to terms with;
You will no doubt adopt and adapt many readings and verses as a Funeral Celebrant. Here is a sample of readings that can be utilized for a Committal: For a non-graveside burial Ceremony;
"*That concludes this part of the ceremony at [place name]. The Funeral procession will now leave for the [cemetery or burial ground name] where the committal will take place.*
For a ceremony held at the crematorium chapel or at a Graveside. Having concluded the readings and tributes we will now move on to the final part of the Ceremony".

The Committal:

The Committal can be an extremely emotional part of a Funeral Ceremony; where the deceased is committed in their casket into the ground. Try not to speak for no longer than 5-8 minutes; because it can be a most solemn and difficult experience for the family and friends of the deceased. There are a number of sample readings for the Committal; Ensure that your words are sensitive and carefully chosen.

The Committal Process:

It can be the most heart-wrenching, so make it formal and brief. A personal choice of the bereaved might be some soft gentle music be played at this stage. The following is a sample of a Non-Religious Committal:

"Please be upstanding. With these tender words we shared amongst us and reverently we commit [first name]'s body to be cremated. We have enjoyed this moment to truly take the time to appreciate for the life that has been lived, and for all that life has meant to us. We were very fortunate that [first name] lived for us to experience all that he has left behind. We have reminisced his words, his deeds and his character here today. We have cherished these thoughts of friendship and most of all we have cherished his love".

After the Committal it is appropriate to ask the mourners to be seated as a final Musical Tribute is played. This will usually be a song the bereaved has chosen.

Closing Words:

Like any meaningful essay that follows the tying up its presentation and to conclude. Soothing words that can bring peace and hope to the mourners; are important to conclude the Ceremony with. Perhaps a non-religious blessing can be given quality, meaning and finality to the Ceremony.

Benediction:

A final spiritual blessing to conclude and that does not necessarily have a religious go-between to reach our Soul. Often Celebrants have been known not to conclude the Funeral service with a religious Benediction; however, it does not always have to end with the Lords' Prayer. A non-religious Benediction can give quality, meaning and finality to the Ceremony. In the same way this kind of blessing can bring comfort; A Funeral poem too can be as sure way of creatively expressing what your loved one has meant and to those who mourn them. There are so many combinations to add from; originally made prayers to non religious blessings; variations of original ideas to synthetic and from others inspiration.

The following is a sample:

"We now leave the memory of [first name] in peace.
To the home she never left and can be found still gardening,
as free as the birds that visit and play around her bird feeders,
as strong as its oak tree that held them. [first name] radiant as the
sun that watches over us, know that you will be mourned and missed;
that no one can replace you; that you have loved and are beloved.
Move beyond form; to all things as the multiverse, feeding on
awareness and Soul reflecting moonlight, radiant as the stars in the
night sky reside, blend with galaxy, and enter into omnipresence;
with love, return to the ocean like a tear drop of life and to steep in
the cauldron of rebirth. With these enduring thoughts and reverence
we bid her farewell. She has left behind the strength and support from
each other to find when sharing in these many fond memories of
[first name], "Rest, heal and grow young again". Be blessed.
We release her in us a worthwhile devotion to all things meaningful
and as real as she had taught us to experience in each and every
moment".

Ceremony for a Stillborn Baby:

A short life, can naturally mean this type of Ceremony will be somewhat shorter (10-20%) and very emotionally stressful to perform for the parents. The challenge is in finding a respectful and meaningful way of coping through this delicate balance between helping the mourners to accept their tragic loss and not it being too patronizing or self indulgent.

The following is an excerpt from a brief sample Ceremony:

"We come here this morning to this beautiful, peaceful sanctuary to commit the body of Rebecca, be still our hearts in this moments passing for Gwen and Peter, having to commit Rebecca to the Earth. Rebecca was a delicate as a butterfly yet like budding flower who never got the chance to open; it is in this hopeful radiance we felt as sunshine and shone inside our hearts..

Baby girl perhaps too soon you came around to breathe, to laugh, or to cry – with us. Gwen, your mother had lovingly nurtured you through those months that you had grown, wriggled, punched and kicked; making your parents anxiously aware that you were waiting to become their little girl. We grieve today for the life that did not come to be and for the life that Gwen and Peter did not get to live with Gwen".

This Ceremony can also be formatted for an Infant.
==REVISED==

FUNERAL CEREMONY DRAFT

FOR

Charlotte Sky Ericson

The following is a complete Bespoke Funeral Ceremony.
It is exclusively formatted as a Celebrant Copy must resemble.

(Front page cover)---

The Funeral Officiant & Ceremony

REVISED
Celebrant Copy:

FUNERAL CEREMONY DRAFT

FOR

CHARLOTTE SKY ERICSON

Monday, February 17, 2014

1:30pm

WeCan,
Cremation Centre

FUNERAL CEREMONY for Charlotte Sky Ericson

Entrance of the casket to the 1950's 'Mickey Mouse Club Theme' song   (2min 41sec)

Mourners to follow casket in and take their seats.
Photo of Charlotte dressed up as Mini Mouse crouched down posing as a little mouse on her 2nd birthday~ 3 days before first treatment prominently displayed.

Good morning and welcome; please be seated now.
I am a Funeral Celebrant my name is Maria Arvanitidis and I will be conducting the Funeral Ceremony of Charlotte Sky Ericson. We are gathered here today to mark the loss of a life yet to unfold and the hardest most unimaginable grief experience for anyone to go through. On behalf of her family and dearest friends here today I want to send out my deepest sympathy.

On December 21, 2013 Charlotte Sky Ericson died at the age of 2 and a half from a rare strain of Leukemia at Sick Kids Hospital. Adam and Mary-Jane, our deepest sorrow goes out to you.
To Charlotte's grandparents; Sandra Stavanger; Jane Ericson and "gangad James" was how she called her grand father; both her aunts, Emily & Kristen ; Adam's and Mary-Jane's closest of friends Aaron & Amy.

As well to all the caring people here today who have supported them through this heart-wrenching time in their life, our thoughts are with you all.

We know that Charlotte would have brought so much love into this world, and has done so already, and you have been part of that love with your positive feelings, your caring, your concerns and in strength of your unity in family and friendship.

Adam & Mary-Jane are so grateful for the many more dedicated friends and family here with us; who gave emotional and practical support during this difficult time. They want to also thank the staff at Sick Kids Hospital, whose devotion to little Charlotte and wonderful care was truly appreciated.

On behalf of her family, we would like to invite every one to join us after this Ceremony here at WeCan cremation Centre back to Adam's and Mary's house for refreshments; at 1 Dingle Dell street.
There are no words of comfort that can adequately cushion the shock of losing this precious child. The cluster of emotions felt are coming forth to be experienced and do not have to be explained, rather expressed out for little Charlotte.
Let's commence now with this poem called
"Please Don't Ever Tell Me"

3.11 min.

The Funeral Officiant & Ceremony

reading

I'm going to tell you something
I hope you'll never have to know.
I'll tell you how a heart can break
And tears can constant flow.

I lost my baby girl you see,
An angel in my eyes
God chose to take her hand one day
And led her to the skies.

But please do not forget my child
She was a person too
And forever she will live
Inside of me and you.

So, please don't ever tell me
That time will heal my pain
Because not even time
Can bring her back again.

Just tell me she is happy
In that land way up above
She's snuggled in an angels wings
All wrapped in Mommy's love.

Author Unknown

53 sec.

Eulogy

Mary-Jane Stavanger now 25 and Adam Ericson 27 had both joined the Royal Navy; where they both met in June 2010 and became shipmates. They Started living together for a couple of years; when Mary-Jane found out she was pregnant. With Charlotte on the way now; Mary gave her notice and left the Navy while Adam continued on with it.

On May 21 2011 the day of Judgment as predicted by most religious affiliations; posting with great fear for all the end of time is near.

Charlotte Sky Ericson was born this day at Mount Sinai Hospital Old Toronto. She was a perfect healthy baby and at about a half an hour after Mary Jane's water broke Charlotte came out. Shortly afterwards and in June of 2012 Charlotte's mother gave birth yet again this time to her little brother Freddie Eric Adams.

Charlotte learned to talk well before she was one year old and her first words were "gangad". Her grandfather thought it sounded like "grand-dad" and although her mother sais it is "dad"; her granddad has never corrected her since because he liked to hear her call him "gangad".

Precious Charlotte like many other children loved to watch television programs such as the ever popular pre school series In The Night Garden and as much as she liked to watch Sponge Bob Square Pants, she did not like the character Ben 10. Charlotte did however like all things of Walt Disney especially Mini Mouse.

She knew how to count to 30 and by being an avid fan of Mini Mouse learned the alphabet from The Mickey Mouse Club.

Just before Christmas of 2012, her grandpa James made a six foot drawing of Mini Mouse all dressed up in red. How funny it was when Charlotte would shut the lights out the dress turned pink and would glow; she liked this so very much.

The Funeral Officiant & Ceremony

Charlotte was a forceful little red head; one time she even tried to get her granddad to eat a cake made out of toy slime and he was devastated. She liked to bake cakes with her mother and both grandmothers and as a direct result of this would make them out of anything she played with like sand; Play-dough and even Lego-bricks.
In and around May 2013, when she started kindergarten; there too she loved to play in the sand box to make fairy cakes with the sand; insisting her fellow pupils to eat them and stood and watched until they did so.

Very quick witted her teacher even gave her the nick name "Chatty Cathy" named after a doll she had growing up; with a cord you would pull from the back to make her talk because Charlotte was a real chatterbox.

At kindergarten is where she had started to try to read with the help of her teacher Martha who knew Charlotte as a very loving and contemplatively thoughtful child in all things.

From watching the Mickey Mouse Club and after her loving "Gangad's" drawing of Mini Mouse on her bedroom wall we can only begin to imagine how much she loved Mickey and Mini Mouse.
In the summer of 2013 Charlotte's parents took her for a family vacation just outside of Paris to Euro Disney.
Along with Mary's and Adam's friends they spent 5 fun filled days getting to know and make friends with Mickey and Mini Mouse.

Sweet adorable little Charlotte even asked Mini Mouse "if she would like to come home with her " and Mini responded by saying "she would love to but she had to stay there".

About the end of June after getting back from her wonderful vacation, the blood disorder that was detected just before her second birthday; was now actually diagnosed as a rare form of Leukemia.

Her entire family went through heroic measures; however with all the tissue sampling, nothing could come close to a match.

It was such a rare strain that not even a match for a bone marrow transplant could have fixed it permanently.

Like all children in and around Charlotte's age; living in a different more magical fantasy like world and where everything is so much larger than life. We appear God like to them; with our many talents and experiences, we offer surely is not taken for granted by them. Every little detail mystifies them in awe as they feel our connection to them grow and they stand watching us care for them like avatars.

I would now ask for every one's attention while we invite two of her dearest loving avatars: in tribute to our beloved Charlotte
Nana Sandra and Grandpa James are going to share a few words; with a reading of a short Inuit proverb and a poem Written by a pediatric nurse, and as submitted to a newspaper columnist somewhere in the mid 19th century(both reads have adapted and revised for this publication).

<u>When Words lose their concept:</u>

5.19 min.

The Funeral Officiant & Ceremony

<mark>Nana Sandra:</mark>   <u>When Words lose their concept</u>

~ How can I say, "I can feel exactly in the way of this particular loss"
when I can only come as close as to imagine.
I feel but only the sadness of my child missing hers.

~ I can't take this away from her experience, with shallow words
   that say "get over it and suck it up"- because this is her grief.
   Life will keep progressing to not consider it as much.
   She will have to sail with these emotions, a midst her daily
   common routine. The distractions can help, but never to fully
   comprehend these thoughts and feelings from within her mind.
   Maybe the hurt will slowly dull enough to cope.

~ Until that day, the words are inconceivable, that kind of
   love and comfort from your son, is not to be expected
   because he can never be replacing her —no one can.

~ I can't say, "forget about it", and just have another on that slim
   chance of her coming back, either. She is irreplaceable
   and anything other in this way of thought, is simply an escape,
   from all those sleepless nights. I cannot find for any surface chatter
   to express; but how I feel right now to find you in this place.

~ That "I am here. I care and as my daughter's daughter that you
    are to me. Perhaps your broken heart can mend
    and for as long as this grief lasts; "I will talk about
    your daughter and listen and maybe some day we can laugh
    about these memories.

~ I don't know how you feel nor can I tell you to get a grip,
   but I can learn a little more as you mourn and of what
   you are going through each time.

~ In every day from here on by, I hope that you can start
   to feel a little lighter from this burden that we all here share.

                                                    1:27 min.

Gramps James :   An Inuit Proverb

"Are they not stars,
these openings to heaven
Portal remnants and where the love of our lost ones
flaring down and through our thoughts illuminating us
with joy and happiness".   16 sec..

Thank you James and Sandra; how very appropriate as our little
star Charlotte. She would have wanted more than anything, one of
her favourite nursery rhyme's Twinkle Twinkle Little Star; for those
who feel to sing along or just listen
and reminisce while the music plays on.

.22 sec.

The song Twinkle Twinkle Little Star Rhymes
(by Jane Taylor 1806)songs starts playing now

3 min

Twinkle Twinkle little star, how I wonder what you are.
Up above the world so high
Like a diamond in the sky
Twinkle Twinkle little star, how I wonder what you are.
When the blazing sun has gone.
When he nothing shines upon
Then you show your little light
Twinkle Twinkle all the night
Twinkle Twinkle little star, how I wonder what you are

I would now ask for every ones attention while we invite
Charlotte's Aunty Kristen to share with us a poem called
"The Elephant in the Room".

.25 sec.

The Funeral Officiant & Ceremony

The Elephant In The Room

There's an elephant in the room.
It is large and squatting,
so it is hard to get around it.
Yet, we squeeze by with,
"how are you" and "I'm fine..."
and a thousand other forms of trivial chatter.

we talk about everything else
except the elephant in the room.
We all know it's there.
We are thinking about the elephant as we talk.
It is constantly on our minds.
For you see, it is a very big elephant.
But we do not talk about
the elephant in the room.
Oh, please, somebody say my child's name
Oh, please, say it again
Oh, please, let's talk about the elephant in the room.
For if we talk about their death,
perhaps we can talk about their life.
Can I say their name...
and not have you look away?
For if I cannot,
you are leaving me alone...
In a room...
with an elephant.
~Author Unknown

1:03 min

Thank you for sharing those words with us Kristen!   .10 sec

The Committal words

All rise now please, if you can; as we give our final blessings to send off Charlotte Sky Ericson.

She was a little ray of sunshine that danced and shone inside our hearts. Her little life has been taken before it even began.

As we commit Charlotte's body to be cremated; there is no point in searching for meaning in such a death. For some or all of us may feel anger and pain, while others hurt and deep sorrow that such a thing can happen.

So, whatever happens, let it happen – even the tears and the sorrow. You see, its ok to cry, its good to cry, and it is important to express our love in this way; to speak and think of our precious Charlotte until our sorrow begins to become bearable and slowly heal.
To know this, we begin to find the strength and courage
within our hearts to feel this bravery grow only to find its true meaning; then we can make peace with it.

1:11 min.

Please stand (if you are able).
(Curtain to go over)

The Funeral Officiant & Ceremony

The Committal

We now leave the memory of Charlotte Sky Ericson with enduring thoughts and respect, we bid her farewell.

May we find comfort in your memories of Charlotte and support from each other.

I want to thank you all for the many beautiful flowers that surround us here. There are almost as many of us here as there are the flowers you brought for Charlotte. Unfortunately the crematorium has no place to put them and instead of throwing them out; would make suggestion to take some back with you to the Ericson's family home for refreshments.

Thank you. .40sec

This ceremony has now concluded as I leave you with one of Charlotte's favourite Theme song of The Night Garden by the Cbeebies

11 sec.

PLAY 'The Night Garden' Cbeebies 2 min.

Colour Key
Black – Celebrant
Blue – music
Pink – Verse/poem
Green – other speakers

Total
-→ <u>20.49 min.</u>

To recap: Bringing forward from Chapter I of Page 35 ~ *Preparing the Funeral Service Ceremony before a loved one dies* …All the way to the beginning of this Chapter V about <u>Setting the Tone within the opening of the Ceremony to summing up is the following review guide to sample:</u>

<u>Starting the Ceremony</u>

The Ceremony can start by playing appropriate music; either the choice of the bereaved or by the Funeral Director. To(music will be completely covered in the next chapter)briefly mention it: anything from 5 to 10 minutes prior to the start of the Ceremony whilst the mourners arrive.

<u>An Opening Reading</u>

An opening reading is a matter of choice for the bereaved; with a brief opening reading the ambiance can be created as well as to establish the theme for the Ceremony.

<u>Introduction</u>

"Who and in what character theme are we introducing ?
It is a rare gem to be loved externally and by someone other than ourselves. It's a love that defies description.
A mother' love is not the same as a partner's love and so we come to the many flavours of its intensity and in the same way when it that shadow of such grief to follow. In the many variations of this love for [First Name] we feel it in our hearts this loss".

The Funeral Officiant & Ceremony

Words to Soften Grief

"We grieve today from these memories of [First Name] foremost in our thoughts. Her gain our loss; her happiness our sorrow and yet she would like for us to feel her happiness instead.
The happiness that we all shared in the experience of knowing what we would have missed without knowing her.
To remember her life with respect and happiness. Nothing can disconnect us from this happiness and closeness of [First Name] but our own minds that wish to keep her there unfortunate in the lack of the material physical form we could before touch and prove she was there to each other. It is something to have such an affect on us and us on her we knew as [First Name].
Change can be a good thing when we can allow it to help us grow and love even deeper than before. [First Name] has now transformed into something greater and we too can in this way by knowing just how much we felt this love from her to transform us. Her Love for us is unchanging; it cannot be altered by time, circumstances or even by death. What has been the past and with all its meaning, is in our memories. Be grateful that [First Name] was part of your experience to grow and love just by appreciating this alone and let this feeling of her love expand and grow deeper through us".

Tribute

"As a tribute to [First Name], her daughter [State Her Name] will now share her thoughts with us. Please come forward [State Her Name]".

"Thank you [State daughters name], for those beautiful thoughts and images of your Mother".

Eulogy

Preparation of the Eulogy has been covered elsewhere; however, it can be simply introduced in the following way:
"In this moment, it is our privilege to share with you the life of [Full Name]".

Readings and Tributes

Often Funeral Ceremonies can be non-religious; an elderly deceased perhaps might have some traditional component. How about adapting to something as this ? The "People's Prayer"
For those of you, who wish to, please join in saying

The 'People's Prayer' by RmA

Our loved ones, who art in heaven.
Sacred in our knowing them by name.
Only in their matter have they changed
The unformed be it never obsolete,
This too from within is relevant and unchanging.
When our bodies shed away and our kingdom finds us ready
We will reunite there and so too our bodies will remain
The earth, She will reshape from Soul anew.
As it is in heaven, encased in all the many clusters of stars within the midnight sky awaiting to return again..
Give us this day to forgive and to remember only in the love we have gained by it and be led by those examples.
Remember them as they have known
Deliver us through love
Into thine kingdom
The connection and the brilliance,

Amyn

Music

"As a tribute to [First name] we will now play the beautiful song "Yesterday" by the Beatles, one of [First Name]'s favourite songs While this song is playing, you may wish to turn the pages of your memory like a book, and reflect on the special times you may have shared with [First Name]"

The Funeral Officiant & Ceremony

Readings

There are many useful readings to compose and that can also be made to adapt. Some samples will be provided in the following chapters to come; but for now the following is an excerpt to consider.

"I'd now like to say some lovely and meaningful words to [First Name], on behalf of you, her family and friends.
You gave us your love and a reason to live".

[First Name] your presence was enough to fill the room and our hearts.

In our mind's eye you have forged a place.
We can find you in our dreams and for as long as we can think
and have the feelings to remember
We will, think of you – [First Name]

There is no limit in the place that finds you seeing us and hearing us when we speak of you [First Name]

For now we kiss your cheek
And touch your hand that once could warmly hold us,
We will, remember you - [First Name]

Your warm embrace
And your essence in the things that entertained
Are left behind for sentimental
everywhere and in all things
And that includes our hearts
As long as we have the breath to speak you name
We will love you, [First Name]

Maybe the theme was more to do with the fading away of a suffering loved one from Alzheimer's or dementia; to which another reading might be more appropriate than the above.

Final Tribute

"As a tribute to [First Name], while we play the beautiful melody "Moonlight Sonata" by Beethoven would those who wish to, please come forward and place something that the deceased might want to have taken with them; perhaps a card and/ or flower on the casket, expressing your love and saying farewell".

Committal

"As we have congregated with family and friends around our dearly departed [First Name].
With eyes closed in this world and open to another you have gone and left us to grasp in this awareness.
Others who have gone to join and reunite with from before.
Now you can be with those like us will one day come to join you again in this place and you loved us so.
We will carry you in our hearts every day,
In our thoughts and in our blessings.

A private reflection and a tear or two,
We will always love and miss you.

Go with this appreciation, of you always.
Go with our loving care and leave us in this solace.

Please be upstanding.

With great reverence we commit [First Name]'s body to the ground". We stand here grateful in this moment that we shared together for our beloved [First Name]. We are sad to see her go but happy we have shared in her experience of life. To see her face and feel her hand presence with us here today. We value the memories of her words, her deeds and her character. The friendship we invested in and most of all we cherish her love"

Closing Music

"Please be seated".

"As a final tribute to [First Name] we will now play another of her favourite songs".

Benediction (non-religious)

"We now leave the memory of [First Name] in peace. With enduring love and respect we bid her farewell ".

"May you find richness and example in your memories of [First Name]. May you find strength and support in your love for one another and may you find peace within yourselves".

Chapter VI

SELECTING FUNERAL SONGS:

Music during a Funeral/ Memorial service or Celebration of Life is quite an important factor during Funeral and Memorial services. The appropriate type of music can have a very calming affect on guests, even while the service may be difficult to attend.
Some music during the service is helpful, find something that's suits the service you are preparing and also your loved one. What would the deceased have preferred ?
Pay a attention to the lyrics and what the song is conveying; because it must be suitable for the service. The lyrics and/or instrumental type of music cast the theme and overall mood for the environment as well as having it be appropriate for the gathering of guests. It is also a good idea to choose songs that your loved one enjoyed. Play the music at the beginning while guests are arriving and seating, as well as when the formal part of the service has concluded. Funeral Ceremonies usually have music requested or supplied by the family and friends of the deceased.

Chapter VI

SELECTING FUNERAL SONGS: The Celebrant's role is to prepare an introduction for each piece of music. Cooperation with the establishment staff member is important and to know ahead of time who will be operating the music this must be prearranged on time and on cue. You must also be aware of music copyright issues.

Printing & Copyright Agreement:

This information can be also found on the lower portion of the back of the sample contract from Chapter I. Yet another reason of the importance for a Funeral Ceremony Contract!
A Ceremony Purchaser initializes that they are made aware and "*where this transcript and any other pertaining exclusively for singing and the entirety of this purpose to hold this private function/FUNERAL CEREMONY; copyright holder's permission are not required in this case; however must adhere to prudence of the text and any other above "readings, poetry, excerpts as well as pop music and so on ...require printing; that a copyright exists in creative works for 70 years after the death of the writer(s); that it would then be the clients responsibility to obtain directly from them this permission and/or their appointed agent to be charged a fee.*".

Permission forms can be obtained online for authorizations and further distributions to approve of such intellectual property. The above for copyright permission only applies when wishing to make public Ceremony Scripts and for further collate distributions. Normally the Ceremony Scripts are kept private; made exclusively for the client and for you the Celebrant.
After the Ceremony it becomes a keepsake; however the purpose of the Ceremony Transcript is to better serve the Ceremony Officiant to synchronize the entire flow of the event.

SELECTING FUNERAL SONGS:

The music lyrics to songs can be included in the Funeral programs and copies are issued in many cases with the Funeral Service package. Funeral establishments like to provide as much as they can to encourage guests to sing along(similar to "Karaoke").
Also it can be a good idea to choose songs or music that do a good job of representing your loved one's culture and ethnic background. Another option that can be offered is live music by friends, family and even for children to create on their own (a collection keepsake and just as long as it does not offend anyone).

Organ

Pre-recorded or live organ music will be available at most Ceremony venues. Liaise with Funeral Director for advice.

Committal Music

All the many opinions can be useful to adjust with respect to playing Committal music as the casket disappears from view.
It can detract from the intensity of one emotion for another and or become distracting and annoying; in other cases it can be very calming; but mostly it is to indicate that moment where the guests must depart from the venue. The right kind of music can take away some of the harshness of the moment by making it more bearable. This is a matter of taste and one for the bereaved to decide.

After the Ceremony:

Upon completion of the Ceremony, the Funeral staff will takeover. Give the family best wishes; present them with a transcript of the Ceremony and congratulate the speaker(s). Thank any singers / musicians, and venue staff.

These are the little details with regard to a healthy public professional perception. Practice to pitch in with the Funeral Directors and staff, to show a willing helping hand never hurt anybody and it reflects well on team spirit.

Do not be afraid to ask from them an evaluation and act on their feedback when they do.

After 1 week, make a follow-up call to the family and ask for feedback. Build a website where they can be directed for testimonials or even memorial notices on the deceased.

All of which will help to develop a practice in a professional sense as well as business.

Advertising/Marketing:

Roughly 65% of your business must rely on public relations and getting your services out there. Social media/Flyers/Brochures: Can also help to advertise and further explain what you are offering. The following tri-folded brochure describes some services and can free up your web site domain for other things; like prices, reviews, videos and social media links.

These brochures and leaflets are a great way of meeting your collaborating associations. Meeting with Funeral establishments Radio announcers and other such like minded affiliates; that can all benefit to work well together for clients and to help build a strong community connection. Do not feel threatened by those already established in the spotlight; a pushy image savvy of importance, from having reviews; testimonials and raising the bar yet to another level. Not everyone is gadgetry inclined or software know it all's; simply take comfort to know we all have to start somewhere, learn to have compassion and be patient !

The Funeral Officiant & Ceremony

The Funeral Celebrant

The mission is to create what best reflects of your loved one's wishes and designated family and friends; - cultural background, beliefs, and values.

The Celebrant takes the time unhurriedly to spend with you; how to best collaborate a carefully crafted eulogy and create a Ceremony with music, quotes, readings as well as any other rituals and unique symbols that your Celebrant will need to be informed of. The Ceremony can only be delivered after every detail and of the eulogy is checked and approved by you.

The Ceremony can then be Officiated by the Celebrant at any given venue of your selection. After the funeral and/or memorial tribute, the Celebrant presents your family with a beautiful copy of the Ceremony as a keepsake. Although nothing can really take the grief away; we are here to help provide an authentic and well prepared tribute that may ease the pain.

EVERY LIFE HAS MEANING !

How long is a Ceremony ?

A typical Funeral Ceremony at any Centre lasts roughly 40 minutes

From the arrival of the deceased to the departure of the mourners from the chapel. The rates however on most cemetery and crematorium chapels price lists normally range from 30 minutes to a full hour. A Celebrant may actively be officiating for the whole 40 minutes; however will be talking only 20 to 30 minutes(for a double slot booking the full hour). The remaining of the ceremony is taken up by music, and perhaps other speakers.

Also made available: an offer to prepare as good practice a full eulogy, even when a mourner is the main speaker. This will ensure that even when "speaker" falters the Funeral Celebrant can step in. After the main speaker(s) finishes, the Funeral Celebrant can then summarize to ensure all the requested information is imparted.

All these factors affect the length of a Ceremony

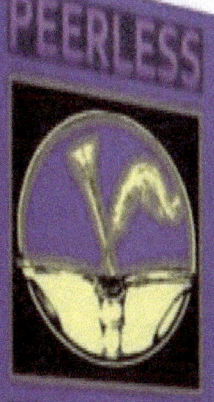

PEERLESS MOMENTS

What does a FuneralCelebrant do ?

To deliver with confidence, care and sensitivity, a properly prepared Bespoke Ceremony. For a Complete and elaborate version to draft, requires 3to5days notice from being appointed Carryout an initial interview with the bereaved for an outline of the Ceremony and gather all relevant information. Then to write/ rewrite and revise the Ceremony.
It is our responsibility to methodically record the details of your deceased loved one's life story.
What is written must depict the true character of that person. To create a portrait from the information gathered; to better reflect from family and friends about their most cherished memories of the deceased.

Collaboration

- Some religious Funeral Ceremonies can have to provide a Homily; and is added to the fixed formal Liturgy set in place. On average the price for a church service alone is far too costly. The idea of combining a Ceremony with a Celebrant and Clergy member at the Funeral; Cemetery chapel centre chapel; legion hall and/or any major community centre; or venue and makes for at half the cost.
- A Secular and/or Semi-Secular non-denominational Civil Celebrant can work in collaboration with Clergy and Funeral Director combined; to fully integrate with your wishes at heart.
- Although Celebrant Funerals tend to be Secular(non-religious) A moment of silence is common.
- The deceased too might have had spiritual views that certain prayers can be offered to connect with ; Maybe "The Lord's Prayer" and/or The 23rd Psalm ?
- Humanists from an Atheist stance will support Secular and scientific;
- In between a religious service or a Humanist one is the Civil Funeral; driven by wishes, beliefs and values of deceased and their survived by.
- A good Funeral Ceremony is unique; focuses on the life of the person who can no longer continue physically and in praise to them; is spiritually this moment in memory of.

Pre-arranged Funeral Ceremony

The marking of a very important event and A VERY WISE SELECTION

- A commemorative event can be held wherever and whenever.
- For those wishing to have a Ceremony. The Funeral usually takes place within a few short days. For this reason it is wise to go with a " Pre-Planned Ceremony" package; that can easily be revised.
- During the time you decide with a Funeral home to pre-arrange your Funeral. Why not opt to take the time likewise for your Ceremony too.
- A "Free Thinker" might want to contribute in his/her very own Ceremony before hand as well.

Secular Service Sample

- MUSIC: something in the beginning; maybe during the middle and at the end; not lasting more than 3 min. for a half hour ceremony!
- After the first piece of music ends A warm welcome is given to all.
- Selected Reading(poetry if desired)
- Tribute/memorial portrait/eulogy, (music) – Personal Memories shared.
- Bell Ceremony: A ringing of a bell to mark the passing of the beloved and to join in silent prayer or moment of silence.
- Closing words(committal).
- Closing Music
- Invitation to reception.

Funeral and/or Memorial

- From A "Graveside Service" (15-20 min.) Ceremony package; And/or A "Chapel Service" that is followed by a "Graveside Burial". What these always have in common is the body of the deceased is always present. With a "Memorial Ceremony" service the body is not present.
- At a Burial/"Committal" held after the main Ceremony at the Chapel, the Celebrant will speak usually no longer than 5-8 min. at best.
- A "Memorial" package is also ideal for a family that decides for a very private and/or "Direct Cremation" or "Burial Service". It makes for an occasion that allows for everyone to say good bye; with love, peace, and dignity. At this time it is urged to Celebrate the life once lived rather than what has been lost; in a way that helps everyone to focus on what has been gained from knowing the deceased. Uniquely so created even with cremated remains present.
- A Memorial service offers the opportunity for a most satisfying personally fitting for all to say farewell. Although an alternative to a conventional Funeral service that is really not all that necessary. Some people prefer both and this too Can be made possible.

Celebrant Officiate: Maria Arvanitidis
peerlessmoments.com ~ 416-920-5464

The Funeral Officiant & Ceremony

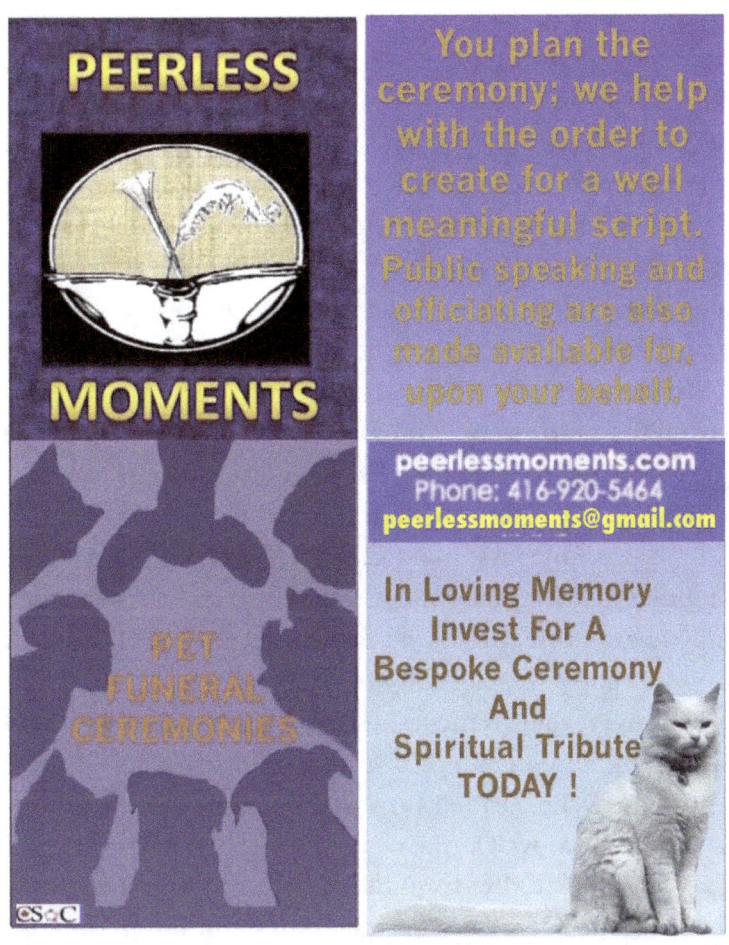

To Further Elaborate:

Review the main part of the Funeral proceedings as mentioned before and let there be no misconceptions; however with a Ceremony anything goes and the sky is the limit. The main part of the Ceremony as is customary, can include a tribute, eulogy; as well as some readings and/or can be broken up into their very own segments as separately having to do with more than one Ceremony for the entire service. These Ceremony services are more elaborate in nature and can incorporate all within one Ceremony; harmonizing such a combination can take over the normal 20 minute script and that of its entirety of 40 minute service proceedings. This is where we are as Celebrants complying with clients and families alike to come to a negotiable agreement and without religious/traditional restraints preferably. It can become paramount to work collaboratively with all team players; including the Funeral staff responsible for the Funeral arrangements. Consider this level of secrecy and of who we are protecting and one in the same as client privacy and confidentiality. The sharing of such relevant information for the Ceremony; rather in these matters is on the focus that veers toward the time constraints and overall structure; it can be very helpful as to the various slots and venues (visitations/wakes and chapel service as well as the committal service and/or the place of Benediction). Another imperative is the coordinating of a Theme. The "Theme" can have the Celebrant coming in dressed like a Star Wars character and Storm troopers leading the way in the procession. It might have the Celebrant dressed up in their pajamas; for a Pajama Party theme. What might be collaborated from imagination versus military and public service uniformed tradition and/or the collaborating with a careful blend of co-creating far fetched and untraditional Markab speakers. Making a difference will prevail for future Celebrants, no matter.

The Funeral Officiant & Ceremony

To Further Elaborate:

The Ceremony Officiant will script the program most appropriate; that can allow for special people to speak and musical selections that can be played. For example: "[*The Graveside Service Package(ChapterVI of page 149)* D] from Peerless Moments pricing samples". This Ceremony can go up to 20 minutes in its capacity; to go beyond, will take it into another pricing package consideration. With some exceptions clearly, these Funeral Packages, from the "STANDARD" to the "COMMITTAL/BENEDICTION". They do not have to be as the name suggests; rather more importantly in the duration of the time and amount of work that is put into completing the Ceremony. A poem or reading is a lovely way to open; then perhaps a photo tribute of 35to50 slides and depending on the length of the song. So many times the witnessing of untimed programs can actually take up more time as they repeat themselves once over. As Ceremony Officiants, we must get the timing as it will be reflecting on our overall performance to conduct and introduce the speakers. It could be a family member discussing their youth and growing up, a close friend, and/or a business associate. Anything from one person speaking the entire time, for ten to fifteen minutes; Or three to five people each speaking, 3-5 minutes at a time and of various aspects of the life of the deceased. When determining the structure, there are 3 things to remember: The significance of the loss, and how much that loved one will be missed. 2) The significance of the person and/or pet who has died; their life, what they did, and the sharing of Anecdotes. 3) Establish the social significance of their loss; who were the others that this loss affected; that this loss touched and how; the tremendous value that they gave to the community and tribe as well as family.

Funeral Ceremony and Children:

Children have a huge capacity for imagination; especially under the age of seven. From seven and beyond to puberty, becoming more withdrawn, seeking out their own identity.
In the same way traditional values are taught to children; we too can learn from their imagination and brainstorm drafting. Include children as much as they are to participate with their ideas, to help build upon a Ceremony. Older children, will be measured on their traditional cultural values and to what extent they can behave, to fit in well with others. Indoctrination opposes imagination and the younger children are, the less these filters are established. They will say exactly how they feel and perhaps come off as nonsensical. To what level of tolerance the adults around them might have and to how much a child can accept without rebelling, is this delicate balance. Explaining and sharing; as much as your relations with them to interact; explore and expand alike together. For example, children might better accept that grandpa is in the other room and *"one day the wall will crumble; then we can be together again; but not in the same way as how we see him now to be"*. Teach the children as much as they are willing to consider and with these very same tools of Ceremony, get them to participate. Explain to them on their level and less pushy from your own societal perspectives. *Ceremony is a great way to exercise the grief right out of us and through self expression "can you help with that?"* The younger the child is, the less emotions it had time to explore and when forced it might feel awkward having to fake it. Encourage them through life to stay open with their feelings and to express them always in any way they can. Maybe Grandpa John was known for always having Chiclets in his pockets.. that held two pieces of gum in each packet, and that is what your child will miss the most ?
You know your children best; however never push them to accept and/or participate beyond their comfort zone !

The Funeral Officiant & Ceremony

Funeral Ceremony and Children:

Children realize that facts are formulated opinions, in that they aren't as they appear; they have not been taught how to believe and in what is real and why that is. In other words, the younger they are; they will see and hear and talk to grandpa still, like he never left the room. The older they become, children will start to ask and feel the loss for any physical attachment. Trauma on the other hand is very much something that and from our very first breath into this world that we experience. The snipping off of the umbilical cord and not allowing the placenta to fall away naturally by drying up. Then the separation from the mother and so on and so forth; creates many traumatic imprints for a child to say the least; numbing feelings and disconnect; the thought of needing others to complete us and so many other factors that we all must as a society work through. Addictive personalities and the lack of love that drives us, is this not a crucial component toward creating grief? The latching on and clingy behaviour of a child; neglected and neglecting parents; the feeding off of a co dependent society as survived; rather than as thriving inter dependent and co creative. This is the difference between a controlling disconnected world; from a loving and accepting connected one. Who is really the adult and who is the child? Who is the teacher and who is the student? Be flexible in this psychology of grief; it can be tricky as the mind will make it and just as difficult of its consult. To recap children from age of 7yrs old and up will experience grief and loss like any other adult would; the more attached to the material and physical existence, naturally the harder and more difficult it is to accept its loss.
The emotional attachment of these things and how meaningful and relevant they shape us into being ? Unable to conceptualize the facts by simply not understanding them as real and to be meaningless, is the other, under the age of 7. These intense emotions can perhaps be noticed even more with a child's pet. Creating Ceremony for their beloved pets is one sure way to start!

ACIFC CSOC

<mark>Client Copy</mark>

FUNERAL CEREMONY

FOR

<u>Gemma The Cat</u>

Saturday on August 5th

12pm/noon time

Holy Pets Cemetery Graveside Service

1974 Concession Road RR1

The Funeral Officiant & Ceremony

FUNERAL CEREMONY for Jessica's CAT GEMMA

Upon arrival at the Graveside Ceremony to begin with a poem:

<u>Gemma</u>

Love has no bounds

pouncing on us reckless

Like a playful cat

on haunches hunting yarn balls

and playing with the string \

She left no house plant gone un chewed

The favoured chair of hers that she had clawed away,

now left behind and shall remain in memory of her last sign in.

~ maria

Good afternoon my name is Maria Arvanitidis, and I am the Celebrant that Jessica has trusted to carry out this Graveside Ceremony. I would like to welcome all of you here, and out from your busy schedules that no words can describe. This meaningful support does bring to help Jessica and in sharing the loss you must all be feeling uniquely, alongside her to comfort each other with.

Gemma was not an outdoor cat, but on this particular day of Monday afternoon of July 31st, 2017 she was let out.

Unfamiliar to her surroundings and not too far did Gemma stray and things got really crazy very quickly after that.

In that same instance during the late afternoon Jessica's dear pet and companion Gemma tragically passed away by this unfortunate accident that had taken place.

When Gemma had made for her escape to run after the neighbour's dog and without a leash he instead turned and barked at her. She got so scared, she ran out onto an oncoming car in such great panic. Jessica was there to witness the whole accident right before her eyes and before she could do anything; as she could recall, it happened far too quickly.

The person in the car after coming to a screeching stop over their vehicle got out to see what happened. Jessica quickly ran toward the car but much to both of their dismay the accident was too unavoidable. The person who hit Gemma with their car is here with us today and has felt so badly about being so distracted at the time to not avoid to swerve from running over Gemma. The only way that felt befitting enough for them; was to volunteer to cover the cost for Precious Gemma to be buried here at Holy Pet cemetery and where Jessica had chosen.

If Gemma could converse with God; and we could to hear them; the following words could not have better described as in this here "Poem For Cats" by an unknown Author.

The Funeral Officiant & Ceremony

<u>Poem For Cats:</u>

And God asked the feline spirit Are you ready to come home?

Oh, yes, quite so, replied the precious soul And, as a cat, you know I am most able To decide anything for myself.

Are you coming then? asked God.

Soon, replied the whiskered angel

But I must come slowly
For my human friends are troubled

For you see, they need me, quite certainly.

But don't they understand? asked God
That you'll never leave them?
That your souls are intertwined. For all eternity?
That nothing is created or destroyed?
It just is....forever and ever and ever.

Eventually they will understand, Replied the glorious cat
For I will whisper into their hearts That I am always with them

I just am....forever and ever and ever.

Author Unknown

Born on February 14, 2009. Gemma a Domestic Short Hair cat; had lived for about 8 years.

Unbeknownst to having any owner prior and before her adoption from Jessica; was found roaming the streets by the Humane Society. When the Humane Society had picked her up; she was strong and healthy to have a local pet store take invested interest. This local store often had cats from the Humane Society that they would sell for adoption. The money always had gone back to Humane Society. As a charitable contribution that could insure for Gemma's health coverage; all the recommended standards up to date and that of appropriate vaccinations. Jessica wanted an older cat and Gemma was at the time going on five years old; most people do not go ahead and adopt adult cats and in this way she would help to save a cat from such abandonment. Jessica had adopted Gemma for Christmas of 2013 and with a harassing character throughout the three four years that she got to know, but in a good way!

When Gemma was firstly introduced to her surroundings she found that Jessica had also a few birds. Jessica had these birds for roughly five years and it took a very long time to adjust to them. Gemma would stand in the living room in one corner and the birds would be directly on the other corner, where she would dart across and land on the cage where the birds would go lower and try to claw at them. After a while she got used to them and then there were no problems.

The Funeral Officiant & Ceremony

Gemma was a very affectionate cat and as long as Jessica's bedroom door was open, she would come in and sleep right by her head and on her pillow. Before she made herself comfortable, Gemma would do as all cats and claw and knead the pillow.

The pillow she would fluff it up all nice on the side where Jessica lay down her head to rest on and then the purring would put her to sleep. A custom routine that Jessica will sadly miss and has to find other ways to adjust now with her sleeping patterns.

Amongst some of her other good and not so good idiosyncrasies were; to chew on all of Jessica's plants and often, she would chew on all the leaves. Their was a certain wooden chair near her litter box off to the side. This chair was separate from all the other chairs that were fastened to be placed under the table; she would love more than any other piece of furniture to claw it and claim for as her own to jump and rest on.

Jessica had noticed in Gemma to be a very persistent cat when seeking out attention and she would nudge; nudge and nudge again with her head at people, until she got pated and loved to be rubbed.

Other than a ball of yarn or a string from it that she might play with; Gemma was just a regular cat that had no special toys to claim. Gemma the house cat was Jessica's pampered princess, and mostly preferred her food over any other distraction.

Whenever Jessica was in the kitchen she would take notice of Gemma's presence around her treats that were off to the side, looking at her meowing and there she waited patiently. Sometimes she would become very crafty and when Jessica was not paying attention; she would knock the treats right over, only to figure out a way to open them. Aside from loving her cat treats very much; Gemma was not a fussy eater and would eat anything, mostly to do with salmon fish and chicken.

One thing that Jessica found most peculiar about Gemma and aside from drinking it out of the toilet; that she hated running water. When she would sense running water anywhere that included from the kitchen faucet, running in the sink or in the bathroom she would dart away. For this strange reason and because Gemma did not like the sound of water; Jessica would never attempt to wash her and instead would take her to a groomer. Gemma had become not only part of the family but also did not take too very long to ripple out her love and into the hearts of the entire family and friends who are here today. Jessica has asked it that we take a moment to just be silent and personally reminisce in the ways that Gemma might have touched your lives. To the duration for this time, a requested Cello piece of instrumental music, will play within the background by "The Piano Guys" called Rolling in the Deep~ by Adele

(Piano/Cello Cover) - The Piano Guys   4min.

The Funeral Officiant & Ceremony

When left alone, Gemma would often wait by the windows. Gemma's habit was made very clear to rest on by the windows and wait for the hours before Jessica would get home from work. Finally when Jessica and having not too far to enter in the house, would notice Gemma looking at her from the window and; Gemma too could notice her. Just before the door could open ajar; Gemma would be there to greet her, right in front of the door. She would welcome everyone first thing this way and likewise to greet them at the door. How she would recognize them all it still remains a mystery. Gemma was a very simple average looking cat with lots of soul; that everyone would right away warm up to. She had a keen sense and very alert; when someone would decide to spend the night. She would go between the rooms to sleep close by them for attention. During some rare occasions her younger sister Amanda would come to house sit and look after Gemma. Jessica's younger sister Amanda, is here with us to feel this loss right next to Jessica like as her very own.
Amanda felt somewhat of a closer resonance with Gemma.
They would often joke about and for this reason to why she trusted her to house sit.

Since Gemma was adopted Amanda had become quite fond of her when she was five; because in cat years relative to human years it would equal to about the same age as herself.

Gemma would show for much affection and was cradled on the lap from mostly all her family and friends as she was a very friendly cat. In her own way the protégé of unconditional love for all inclusively that would be opened to her and likewise equally to respect the space of those who did not feel for her in such a way. Gemma was a very sensitive and understanding well to pick up in advance the personality of others. This is what made her special and the personality of a well adjusted socially interactive house cat.

She would always engage as her playful self when guests dropped by to pay a visit and as much as they would allow. Gemma was always Jessica's cat and this special bond of recognition was very prominently noticed between the two of them. Before we commit Gemma's body to be laid to rest beneath the earth; I would like to say a few departing words.

I would like to read off one last poem by an unknown author called

"SOMEDAY":

The Funeral Officiant & Ceremony

SOMEDAY

Sometimes when you're feeling sad,

When all you want is me,

I softly jump and curl up in a ball upon your knee.

Some nights when your heart does ache,

Worn out by tears you weep,

I quietly lie and softly purr

To calm you as you sleep.

Somewhere far beyond this place,

A land where all are free,

I'm calmly watching over you,

And waiting patiently.

Someday when the time is right

Your voice will call to me,

And once again I'll softly jump

And curl up on your knee.

The importance of a decent burial within a pet cemetery that brings us here to this gathering is exceptional in helping with the mourning of this dearly departed friend and most loved creature Gemma.

We now leave the memory of Gemma in peace.

With such importance and respect, we bid her farewell.

May we find comfort in knowing that she has been given a decent burial that brings us here today in fondness of her memories that rather than flowers, we can like to donate to the Humane Society and/or at the local pet store where Gemma was adopted.

Thank you all for your presence here to witness Gemma's Ceremony!

Thank you,

Maria Arvanitidis   PEERLESS MOMENTS

The Funeral Officiant & Ceremony

Pet Funeral: Common Elements:

Candle Lighting: By including a simple candle lighting; it can be an appropriate way to symbolize the spiritual nature of the Ceremony.

Prayers and Blessings: It does not have to be a "Benediction", an appropriate adaptation to a prayer and as a blessing may be included.

Poems, Readings, and Songs: Can be used to express your feelings about the loss of your pet and characterize the nature of the pet's life. Songs and lyrics just like poems and readings can be adapted well and/or just left as they are popular.

Sharing of Memories: Telling a story about your pet and its relationship to your family can be uplifting and most cleansing to the soul. It will also give you the chance to share your feelings and introduce some humor into the Ceremony. Consider asking others to also share their memories.

Memorial Photographs and Videos: People often display photos of their pet which represent the spirit of the animal.
The location of the Ceremony might allow for video footage of the pet interacting with family members.
Create a shrine at home to contain an urn with the pet's ashes and photos or other memorabilia.

Maybe Encourage donations to an organization that benefits animals?

Closing Goodbye:
A pet Funeral or Memorial service is just one of the ways you can honor your pet. End the Ceremony by giving a final farewell. Memorialize your pet.

For your beloved Pet and Some Considerations:

Adoption can be a very personal decision. For some, the grief will be transitory. For others, it will take some time to heal. There are no quick fixes for making the pain we feel when we lose a beloved pet. There can be many applications to help cope with the grief over pet loss. Do not apply pressure to the getting over grief with a timetable. Take care of without any real expectations but to set an intention for self care and nourishment. Nurture the physical as well as the emotional needs; where the loss can be felt allow it to surface and when the time is right make note: Do you remember what you treasured in particular of their personality; what was it about them, that was most annoying ? Did they have a weakness or an oddity and what about them made us feel strong and secure inside; that we were loved and felt important ? Perhaps a special language that you shared together? How did your very special friend touch your heart?

From the moment these beautiful creatures come into our life; Perhaps journaling each and every special memory.
After they have passed revisiting can help to comfort for the sinking in loss; it can also be of further assistance to create a very meaningful Celebration of life and/or Memorial Service.

On the other hand unexpected or sudden loss; something as traumatic as a motor vehicle accident or an attack by another animal. Acknowledge in anyway possible these emotions that interdependently were and in the exchange of this relationship.

The Funeral Officiant & Ceremony

For your beloved Pet and Some Considerations:

Explore this connection with as many interconnected others that had in this way related to your pet. It could be as simple as an open house gathering with mingling and conversation, ask the attendees for tributes and respects be paid by those who wish to speak. Recommend an informal format to ask people who were special to the deceased, ahead of time, maybe they would like to take a few minutes to express these words out loud. Otherwise just to make the time and to prepare a story or two; they can opt for someone else to read out loud on their behalf. The shock possibly might even change to try and justify the loss by leading the way in public educational forums; on the preventative measures and how to protect from other future outcomes in this way of tragedy.

Here are just a few of the other ways to pay respects to a beloved family animal: Post an online Memorial/ Funeral Obituary/Death Notice. Create a special place in the garden with stone or marker infused with the pet's cremated remains; perhaps a portion can be encased in a piece of memorial jewelry or have a diamond or gemstone made out of them.

Donate in your pet's name to an organization that helps animals. Have fireworks created from your pet's remains or have the remains shot into space.

Take a walk along a favourite route the pet enjoyed and plant a tree in your pet's memory. A tree/or shrub planting Ceremony in honour of your pet's life. Scatter the ashes in a pet's favourite location. Have a garden stone or memorial made for your garden. Have a diamond or gemstone made from your pet's ashes.

A natural burial where the loved one is wrapped in there favourite "blanky" or sheet and with their favourite toys. All the guests can help to dig at a special place and take turns shoveling and or pouring dirt to fill. Then artistically create a stepping stone to use as a grave marker.

For your beloved Pet and Some Considerations:

It is important to remember that in planning a Funeral Ceremony it can be exactly what you want and what you think your loved one would have wanted. There really aren't a lot of rules... Perhaps an intimate outdoor fire gathering where each guest can share an Anecdotes (a short and interesting story they shared with this special creature) written on a piece of paper, folded and placed into a container. The container can be passed around as each member picks an "Anecdote" and reads it and then throws it into the fire pit. Finally, a wonderful addition to the closing of the program is with a memory takeaway.
It can be something as simple as a ribbon to wear in memory, a packet of seeds(for a flower bed).

Pet Funeral Ceremonies are not a modern custom, people have Memorialized their pets since ancient times. Holding a pet Funeral may not be for everyone, a simple type of Ceremony or ritual can help us to cope with the loss of a treasured animal friend. Whether you choose burial or cremation for your pet's final disposition, your approach to Memorialization can be true to your religious views or environmental concerns.

A Generic Tribute as an Outline Guide:

Introduction- A quote as an attention getter and followed by who you are and who you are talking about..
Background- What are some applicable accomplishments and other obstacles to validate throughout your loved one's life.
Relationship- Outlining the impact of the loved one's life on everyone and the opportunities of anecdotes that highlight their revered qualities.
What has been learnt as a result of their influence
– what of any real value will be carried forward.
Conclusion- Restatement or summary of key points ending positively.

The Funeral Officiant & Ceremony

From Simple to Elaborate:

A pet loss can be just as painful as losing a human family member. A simple few words might not be adequate enough and perhaps a more elaborate as a human Funeral might be more satisfying. What feels right for each individual, will depend on personal preference. Depending on the regulations(GTA city by-laws prohibit cemeteries) of the area; anything from a simple backyard Ceremony, to a complete engaging recommendation and where the Funeral establishment or pet cemetery can accommodate.

By being given the option of a burial and(local veterinarian) cremation services, these compassionate places can also provide for a fee, caskets, urns and grave markers designed especially for pets. This type of niche is a very limited market(for pet Funeral establishments or a cemetery). Some traditional Funeral establishments(in GTA) might even accommodate requests for pet Ceremonies. Consider inviting the people who were significant to the pet's life and ask them to participate in the planning for a meaningful event. Think about some favourite places that the pet would frequent for the venue. Was the backyard or window seat the spot where you were most likely to find him or her? The beach or the park, perhaps? Hold the event in that spot or bring photos of their special place to the venue. Gather additional photos and memorabilia, like pet toys, so guests can recall favourite memories. Was there a favourite food that held the pet's attention? Consider making that food part of the service.

While there are no hard and fast rules regarding what to include in for a Memorial, there are common elements that many people include. These are similar to those already mentioned and as well for human Funerals. How elaborate or simple is entirely up to the bereaved client and how they would like the would like the Ceremony. Similar to infant deaths in general, these services are much shorter and more casual than other Ceremonies.

Pre-planning:

As mentioned in previous pages throughout this book and with keeping a journal of the special moments; as well as planning ahead can bring a bit of relief. It can help to speed up the process and on the options of having to make complex decisions. Rather than having to focus on the details that come after the death of a pet; what the options are, and how to proceed; it will allow for deeper emotional grieving to take place. Turning to a family member, friend, Clergy, or support group can better guide this outlet for expressing these feelings better. Perhaps a veterinarian can further explore to counsel the type of support services they offer and on what to expect during the pet's last days; as well as with other topics such as Euthanization and how to help the pet remain comfortable.

Who might like to visit with your pet before the time comes? What you would like to do with your pet's remains.

Consider a pre arranged and pre-paid Funeral service:
What establishment would offer such a notion in the first place? What a financial invested benefit this can be; to take financial further interest in such advantages. Preplanning Funeral arrangements are easier to accomplish before a loved one passes, the same is true for preplanning a service for a cherished pet, and why not? Back to the Ceremony and perhaps how to best memorialize your(best friend) pet. Ontario might be a little limited just yet and for a full-blown Funeral Ceremony; however people turn to "Pet Funerals" as part of the grieving process, so why not create a ritual? Creating a ritual in advance can help when the time comes for comfort and closure to say "goodbye". Remember the Ceremony and/or ritual can be revised later on. Loss of pet doesn't mean you have to lose the memories.

Many people find that creating a special Memorial can help in coping with the loss of a pet; because it helps to emotionally express these memories and provide a lasting tribute to your pet.

The Funeral Officiant & Ceremony

Chapter VII

Celebrant Copy

FUNERAL CEREMONY

FOR

John Smitty Smith

Monday 12th June 2017

4:00pm

Odell Funeral Home

Followed by the Graveside Service

Meadow Valley Cemetery

6:00pm

FUNERAL CEREMONY for John Smitty Smith

Walking into music from "Puccini~ Madame Butterfly"
As the Puccin's music fades into the back ground
Everyone with Handout Lyrics can sing along
"Ken Boothe~"Everything I own"
Reggae Funeral Music Lyrics

We meet here today to honour and pay tribute to the life of John Smith, and to express our love and admiration for him.
My name is Maria Arvanitidis, I am honoured for the privilege to officiate this Funeral Ceremony and at best as a Funeral Celebrant; to be conducting this Ceremony on behalf of his family and dearest friends today.

May our gathering allow for some comfort to those of his family and friends who are here and have been deeply hurt by this, his sudden death.

John who to most in here would call him Smitty, wasn't a particularly religious person, but it was thought that his Funeral service could include some religious content and for this private gathering of his closest and most dearest to reflect and as most considerate, kind, and loving person that he was at best devoted to his family.

The Funeral Officiant & Ceremony

Its only natural that we should be sad today, because in a practical sense, Smitty is no longer a part of our lives, "we must die, we know" said a character in Shakespeare, " tis but the time and drawing days out that men stand upon", and so we all come to ponder the life and death of this truly wonderful man; with confused and mixed feelings. For we have a powerful sense of loss; combined with a recognition that; if death must come, it's as well that it's not unduly prolonged, we don't want to see someone we love suffer, so this sorrow; and our sense of the fitness of things; don't sit easily together, one purpose of our proceedings here today; is in some way to try to reconcile those feelings.

On Tuesday, June 6th 2017 John our dearest Smitty had his final breath at Toronto General Hospital. Although Diabetes never really bothered him before it came on suddenly and more than his kidneys could function with the medications he was on.
He passed away peacefully and just shy of his 55th birthday.

On behalf of Smitty's family, and for those who might not wish to attend the Graveside; we would like to invite you to the Celebratory dinner at 89 Mulbery Avenue to gather and to meet up from 7pm to start off with sandwiches and coffee.

At around 8:30pm and after the appetizers the actual formal dinner to be given out will follow. Some of the eulogy and mostly anecdotes were shared more intimately yesterday evening that from it this Ceremony continues on and perhaps a little bit more formal than to include the very same speakers here with us today. When we lose someone dear to us the hurt can be almost unbearable, yet somehow we seem to get through it.

We see that just like Smitty this is not the final destination rather a Journey that we all are on its path to and death one of those markers from which to remember time well spent.

In loving memory of our John his most dearest friend Alex Rodriguez and from having shared so many lovely stories here with us yesterday evening during the wake; he would now like to read a poem written by an unknown Author called, "A Silent Tear";

4.16 min's.

and without further ado, Alex Rodriguez:

The Funeral Officiant & Ceremony

I hide my tears, when I say your name,

But pain in my heart is still the same.

Although I smile and seem carefree,

There is no one who misses you more than me.

When I close my eyes and then I see

All the memories that I have of you

Just sit and relax and you will find

He really is still here inside our very mind.

He would not have wanted for us to cry now that he is gone

For he is in the land of song

There is no pain, there is no fear

So dry away that silent tear

Don't think of him in the dark and cold

For here he is, no longer old

He's in that place that's filled with love

Known to us all, as "up above"

A Silent Tear

1min.

by Author Unknown

Thank you Alex and that was most wonderfully heart felt.

John Smith known as Smitty was born on July 5th, 1962, at Toronto General Hospital to Joanne and Joseph Smith.
John was the first in the family to have him depart so unexpectedly like this. His mother, here with us at 85 and father Joseph who is 92, are devastated with the loss of their second oldest son. John came from a family of three other brothers, Matthew the oldest; Luke the youngest going on 39 years of age and lastly the second youngest Mark at 42.
The brothers did pair off well with each other and this was clearly reflective of their differences of age. At 4 years old Matthew finally had a brother to play with. Matthew liked to practice reading Dr. Zeus books to John while growing up; that later John had up his first by the age of 5 called "The Places You'll Go" and that from there he never put down.
John liked to hang out with Matthew very much; however roughly from the age of 7, during his elementary school years alongside to hang out with them came John's closest and most dearest friend Alex Rodriguez. It was from Alex that John got his nickname "Smitty" as they were in Grade 2 together and their teacher was Mr. Smith one day referred to him as "Smitty" and it stuck with him. Alex became like another brother to the family because he was the only son to a single mother and a sister that Matthew later on had married.

The Funeral Officiant & Ceremony

After his sister's marriage and his mother's passing all that was left was his best friend "Smitty". From St. Augusta elementary school, Alex Rodriguez stood strong by John enough to withstand through the ages and to prove as a real friend who is here today.

John and Alex both had attended Mary Magdalene high then John went on to the University of Toronto to become a doctor.

At not even 25 years of age he fell in love and married.

He later came to realize that his career was not worth sacrificing over a wife and children. The thought of having to give up his valued commitment to his community and family for his wife and future children made him realize what he really wanted. Not even a year of feeling suffocated with demands, that he did not care for and he instead divorced. After separating it was his choice to remain single and was not something he never discussed.

It was so long ago that not even once did her name come up as a reminder and he preferred the single life because it was less stress.

Smitty loved fishing as a hobby and it was not considered as a sport to be competitively in with it. Mostly just on a lazy Sunday morning he would travel to Lake Simcoe Or even West to North Wassaga beach and Muskoka and often where he could spend some quality time out with Alex Rodriguez.

One other thing that John did love were children; he always felt at heart as one of them and with equal footing; however did not want to have any of his own.

The closest he had ever been to fathering was with his niece Jessica from his Eldest Brother Matthew. Jessica he kept near to his heart the most to love and cherish like his very own daughter; it was because she admired him so much and always stuck by him close. Eventually she had impressed upon him so much, so that he could never understand how that she might prefer him over and above, even her very own father, it seemed like at times. John born and raised in the North parts of the city did not stray too far and where he preferred the most to live within the suburbs. On the outskirts of the city was where he lived his life most peaceful and quiet. Having the subway close he traveled on the Toronto Transit line each day downtown to work and back again. Amongst its many advantages the TTC for Jessica was that she loved to run away from home and go visit uncle Smitty. John preferred the bachelor lifestyle and she found him to be really cool and a bit of a playboy with the women.

As the Science nerd that he was; she found her uncle loved Jeopardy on television during the evening to watch the trivia and answer the questions before they could. There was nothing else more satisfying to him than his work and a life of no conditions to restrict his freedom with.

From about his early 20s John was very interested in supporting his community. With a full scholarship in University for doing more than 5000 hours of community service; was granted a scholarship and graduated first in his class at his medical school.

The Funeral Officiant & Ceremony

John went on to becoming an (E.N.T.) "Ears, Nose and Throat" specialist and for 20 years remained strong as one of the top 10 doctors in all of Canada.

From the local hospitals he started with the 5000 hours of community service he never stopped loving and supporting the community since. His time at Sick Children's Hospital were the most memorable part of the 5000 hours where he had done a lot of the time reading to the children.

The books he could recall from childhood that he always loved were Dr. Seuss and these books he would read to the children that were sick to entertain and make them feel better.

I now invite Matthew to read as he once had before an excerpt from his brother John's most favoured children's book.

Let us stop here to reminisce the child at heart within us all and to connect with Smitty.

7.48 min's.

Oh, The Places You'll Go!
by Dr. Seuss

1:13 min.

Thank you Matthew.

Dr. Seuss was the perfect get-up-and-go to move mountains that most resembled Our dearest beloved John Smith's personality just the same to motivate others with. John was a funny; hard-working; uncle to Jessica as she well describes him. She appreciated that he came across to her as being always levelheaded; with no emotional responses; everything was always carefully thought out and done in the best intensions for everyone. He always had a strategy for every plan he structured to commit himself to. For Jessica her uncle was always there for her in advance and any time she needed him as a support system. Jessica would see her Uncle Smitty as a very kind, giving and thoughtful man; he was also one of the greatest role models Jessica has ever had. He always believed in Karma and was a very giving man and never judgmental as he genuinely loved people. His motto "LIFE IS TO SHORT" and "WHEN HARD WORK MEETS OPPORTUNITY".

Made for him as great a protégé as he believed in success to be. These are just some to name off of all the many reasons why she thought of him as special. One major component to his life and where he got his spunk from was from his grandmother's feisty nature. John always praised his Granny's fine dining and to the extent that she would go to please him. Grandmother Mary Henry is present here with us today and at the age of 105 years old moving strong.

The Funeral Officiant & Ceremony

Grandma Mary taught him how to sing, when he would gather around the kitchen to keep her company and could hear the oldies on the radio station back in the day.

John found himself learning a lot about cooking hanging around to help his grandmother. As he was growing up he would listen to the radio that would play rhythm and blues; Jazz, Salsa, and anything his grandma had tuned in to listen was fine by him.

While his Granny sang to pass the time he too would sing along with her; it was when he first discovered his voice and to stand up like a man and speak his truth was all from grandma Mary.

It has truly been a harsh experience to have her most precious and dearest grandson disappear from life before her and any of them who have lived much longer. Mrs. Henry wanted to include in reminiscence and during a moment of silence to have one more last time the chance to sing or listen to the song of "You Are Not Alone" by Michael Jackson.

4. min's.

You are not alone - Michael Jackson
   Lyrics   5.36 min.

Just so unfair to have him taken from us and so soon that although this dedicated song might soothe at most to bring back one last time the memories that Mrs. Henry shared with John and what a privilege it was to have shared here with us.

Before we make are way to Smitty's final resting place and section of the Meadow Valley Cemetery for an outdoor closing at graveside.

John's younger brother Luke would like to close off with this final poem by an unknown author and that we may pay our last respects to light a candle and pass by John's casket.   46 sec.

Crossing Over ………………..by Author Unknown

Oh, please don't feel guilty
It was just my time to go
I see you are still feeling sad,
And the tears just seem to flow.

We all come to earth for our lifetime,
And for some it's not many years
I don't want to keep crying

You are shedding so many tears.
I haven't really left you
Even though it may seem so.
I have just gone to my heavenly home,
And I'm closer to you that you know.

Just believe that when you say my name,
I'm standing next to you,
I know you long to see me,
But I'll still send you messages
And hope you understand,
That when your time comes to
"cross over", I'll be there
to take your hand.   1:45 min.

The Funeral Officiant & Ceremony

Luke that was most lovely a piece and thank you for sharing.

For the remaining part of the ceremony you will each get a candle to light and place by the sand box, that is set up near the casket. During this time the song that John and his grandmother knew so well and love to sing you all are most welcomed to join along or just listen to it in the background by Diana Ross "Remember me". This will give an opportunity to pay your last respects before the casket closes and to make the last view of John's repose openly.

64 sec.

Remember me Diana Ross
Ah, Yeah
Remember me as a good thing
Baby, oh Yeah

3.23 min.

Remember me as a good thing
Remember me

38.35 min.

The Committal words

We are here at the final resting place for John Smitty Smith welcome and please take a rose or any other flower that is past around to give to each and every one of you here present. With this flower you can place on top of his casket before it lowers to the ground. Before we commit John's body to be laid to rest beneath the earth I would like to say a few departing words. He came from a Christian Catholic family and although we had previously mentioned to include some comforting words before now we stand and in the glory of God's presence in the great outdoors let us begin. After hiking up the mountains, the anointed ascended master had sat down with his disciples and suddenly the following words came out of his mouth and to enlighten all here who have gathered:

"Blessed are we from his awareness(so forth)............

....

....

...........Rejoice, that in the afterlife there is a heaven

I will now read an excerpt from the Ecclesiastes 3

To Celebrate the death and resurrection with our Lord and in the name of Jesus Christ to hold John's hand we send him off with the following to let him go but never will he leave our heart he will be remembered.

The Funeral Officiant & Ceremony

Existence has a cycle, and every matter has its moment under the Sun: ……………………………………………..

(And so on and so forth)…………… (excerpt from the Ecclesiastes 3 and as it starts with A careful adaptation to observe,)…………..

We are grateful for the life that has been lived and for the part that life has meant to us. We cherish his friendship and most of all, we cherish his love. The family's requested to include the send off with six doves. Before we start releasing doves; I now invite our final speaker. Smitty's second youngest brother Mark, would like to share out loud to us this short poem called "A Candle To Light" ~ by RmA   4:11 min.

A Candle To Light----RmA

When thoughts remind us of a loved one.

In the back of our mind we see them;

maybe we feel an ever soft whisper

that we might want to hear.

Light me a candle, come see me where I lay;

buried under cold ground my body rests,

This empty shell no longer.

Monumental stone with etchings.

My photo looks to a time of once here again staring back.

Light me a candle, place it inside; on top of where I lay no longer.

My spirit now just like this flame,

Above the earth in its reminder.   52 sec.

    Thank you Mark !

| ACIFC | CSOC |

Dove Release…………..   5 min.

We now leave the memory of John Smitty Smith in peace. With enduring thoughts and respect, we bid him farewell. May you find comfort in your memories of John and strength and support from each other. As you will be aware the family's suggestion was that rather than flowers, they would be delighted if you would like to donate to the Sick Kids Hospital.

Now that John and casket have been lowered to the ground, for those who would like to take turns at grabbing the shovel and take some dirt from the mound to throw on top of him can do so. On behalf of Smitty's family, we would like to invite you to thank you for partaking in the Ceremony and once again a quick reminder of the Celebratory Dinner at 89 Hall Avenue to gather and meet up from 7pm To Start off with Sandwiches and coffee. At around 8:30pm and after the appetizers the actual formal dinner to be given out will follow.

Thank you   1:12 min.

                                                                                             11:05 min.

Colour Key
Black – celebrant
Blue – other speakers
Red – Verse/poem
Green – music

Total time of Ceremony…………
49 min. 45 sec.

How To Write A Funeral Program:

Searching for a favourite poem. That special song.
A favourite Bible passage and/or reading.
After knowing what the reader knows; perhaps just a few more things on how exactly to write a Funeral program might be helpful. Normally Funeral programs are created by the Funeral establishment or the Church; however some bereaved clients might opt for the Celebrant to write the program. Perhaps with some help from this book as a guide a Funeral program, might come easier, and the ability to create a program that can express how unique the deceased loved one was. In case there was anything missed the following can further assist to adapt with the need at hand:

Photo of the deceased
The name of the deceased
Date of Birth and Place of Birth
Date of Death and Place of Death
Date and Time and Place of Celebration of Life
Name of Person who is Officiating
Poem or favourite readings
Short Biography of the deceased
Names of the Survivors
Music and Name of Soloist
Name of the Person or Persons Giving The Eulogy
Photo or Video Tribute
Family expression of gratitude for the gathering of guests.
Internment Details of reception afterwards; Time and Place
Organ Prelude
Invocation/Bible Reading
Hymn Selection
Name of Person or Persons Giving The Eulogy
Name of Vocal Soloist
Benediction
Postlude Music

Prayers/poems/excerpt reads&quote samples:

I am sending a dove to heaven,

With a parcel on its wings.

Be careful when you open it,

It's full of beautiful things.

Inside are a million kisses,

Wrapped up in a million hugs.

To say how much I miss you,

And to send you all my love.

I hold you close within my heart

And there you will remain.

To walk with me through my life,

Until we meet again

Author Unknown~

What it seems I do not have, I have and I am grateful for all the many ways it finds me. ~RmA

Sometimes it can take a lot of work, commitment and tenacity To DREAM BIG. ~RmA

The heart will never seek out for any retribution, it is only in the mind that causes hatred to exist. ~RmA

For each moment of every doubt or confusion, know that it is up to us to keep a window open. ~ RmA

What is perceived as unfair and unjust, it can become so extremely overwhelming that it shatters the very glass that seemingly holds it in. ~RmA

The Funeral Officiant & Ceremony

Prayers/poems/excerpt reads&quote samples:

<u>The Higher Self's Prayer</u> by RmA

My higher self, she leads me to lay

beside still waters and green pastures.

Where all is given and there is nothing left to ask

My soul it is restored on the path of love

I seek no longer in her comforting bosom

Yea though I walk through many a dark night of thy soul's content.

I have no fear as it hath lived on by, before me.

Where there are valleys there are peaks, her soothing voice will

guide me, in my thoughts as quick as lightning, at hand her staff

and at the table she prepared that I may join.

Her presence of inner knowing vision she awakens;

Anointest and ever flowing goodness; at her feet mercy shall follow

me for all the days through and unto resurrection where

I will dwell in thy kingdom of ascended master.

AMYN

Prayers/poems/excerpt reads&quote samples:

A Lily
~by unknown

The world may never notice

If a Lily doesn't bloom,

Or even pause to wonder

If its petals fall too soon

But every life that ever forms,

Or ever comes to be,

Touches the world in some small way

For all eternity

The little one we long for

was swiftly here and gone.

But the love that was then planted

is a light that still shines on.

And though our arms are empty,

Our hearts are filled with love.

With every beating of our heart

You'll always be a part

The Funeral Officiant & Ceremony

Prayers/poems/excerpt reads&quote samples:

Excerpt read by ~RmA(The Sovereign Light~ACIMS[book])

In this moment the space of interest to be present let us give this much and from this light the oneness to awaken in its consciousness, that needs not defending:

With this light freely accept to blast apart the many outcomes of suppression; that once upon a time had taken from any given situation beautiful and turned it into ugly.

These are the disregarded imperfections fearing from their impotence to instigate in others, caring only enough never to be seen.

The echoes of opportunities, let us not flounder them in disregard. With love, and self caring innocence, may we embrace the withered state; that can reveal us most vulnerable, as to dismiss from such importance.

This pain is ready to release, to realize for its beauty
That we can now proclaim to be forgiven and so it is that there is no one but to blame. The innocence within the self awaits, not to defend; but rather to be embraced.

By our own awareness of light and as fully present to connect with love.....

"The day will come when we would rather to look out for one another than compete" ~ maria

For Annual Licensing Renewal Professionals:

This focus is particularly made intentional for the Ontario Funeral Director in mind. Perhaps any other vocational of resonance that might also require time in for training on related topics. This book is designed as a curriculum and can be very helpful to those required incentives of time in proof.

As mentioned in the earlier part of this book a questionnaire has developed in the following manor; that would indicate the book was completed and in its reading of it.

From the moment the book is purchased does not necessarily mean it has qualified the standard online course and/or live course power point guest speaker presentations.

This book was designed to help alleviate the over in the thousands of dollars that one must pay and travel far and wide to find. It can but does not have to offer an online course to further in the days demands the pressure on the time restraints and indirect tyrannical behaviours. This system rather is not damaged goods from its previously held in authorities.

The adjustments will be left up to the reader to decipher and just on how they go about the step by step process will reward them directly every step forward.

Step 1: Sure you purchased the book and for this simply taken into account for your submission as proof. One can report the findings of this book to their licensing renewal authorities. The value in this and from the book's perspective can be taken into account perhaps a good hour or so again that would entirely depend to whether or not this would even validate for anything.

The Funeral Officiant & Ceremony

For Annual Licensing Renewal Professionals:

Step 2: The following questionnaire will certainly guarantee that the reader has not only made purchase of the book but has taken the time to read it just as well.
By answering the following questions in this book
Send to: canadiansocietyofcelebrantss@gmail.com
Upon receiving a copy, the reader will get a written proof of 2 hours toward any Funeral related course/training and for the purpose of their Licence program renewal.

Step 3: Upon receiving an actual Funeral Certificate with Canadian Society Of Celebrants, the reader can qualify again for up to 6 hours(must be asked for). It will be at no extra cost, because the independent work and online presence; as well as the time put into it, will be more than sufficient.
Why 6 hours and not as ridiculous as 24 hours?
For those who must adjust to go and be in a classroom setting that in some cases takes 3 days off their schedule and a quarter off a monthly salary.
There's absolutely no need to go beyond the(F.D.) minimum 4 hour provincial requirement; however should it ever be likely to change, 6 hours is more sensible.

Note: The reader does not have to get the questions right, but must show a proof of copy. When answering these questions think of them as a review; because they will be kept to go back over and as a prerequisite guide toward the process of certification.

The Questionnaire:

Q.1. Is their a difference between a Religious Official and a Celebrant ? True or False
Give at least one reason to why you gave this answer ?

Q.2. What is the Canadian Society Of Celebrants?

Q.3. What is the difference between Secular and non Secular ?

Q.4. What is a "Bespoke Ceremony" and What is a Bespoke
 Ceremony Script?

Q.5. Describe the Ceremony Script comprised components
 (a brief skeletal) from start to finish and how it would look.

Q.6. How important is tradition to a Celebrant Ceremony and what is the meaning of a "Guard of Honour" ?

Q.7. What are some of the key pointers when first meeting with your client?

The Funeral Officiant & Ceremony

The Questionnaire:

Q.8. What are some of the questions to ask while in the flow of collecting data from the initial interview ?

Q.9. What is meant by a Memorial and is it an umbrella term for many other services and Ceremony ?

Q.10. What is the difference between a Memorial and a Celebration Of Life Ceremony ?

Q.11. How can a Funeral Service Benefit from a Bespoke Ceremony ?

Q.12. The day before a Funeral you receive a call from the Funeral Director informing that your client's deceased wife had a son from a previous relationship and that he wants to make a tribute at the Service....Any suggestion?

Q.13. Is it possible to offer a pre-arranged service for a Ceremony and before the person has become deceased?

Q.14. You have been asked by a potential client to prearrange a Ceremony for their elderly mother in hospice care and who is suffering from Alzheimer's disease ?
What will be your advice and what type of Ceremony can you recommend, if any ?

Chapter VIII

WHERE DO WE GO FROM HERE ?

You have successfully made it through this book's reading achievement. Welcome to the next stage of the process; to gain certification. If you wish to continue and haven't already done so, a hard copy of this book, is the prerequisite.

Step 1: email the following to,
canadiansocietyofcelebrantss@gmail.com
Your name as you prefer to have it show on the certification and your place of residence address for proper mailing of an authenticated sealed and approved by the CSOC. Please include a telephone contact number; email and/or other, such as "Skype name". Upon request: further training and tutoring package of preference. "The Intermediate Learners" package, is Phase (1) & (2); or "The Advanced" package, Phase (2).

The Intermediate package; to conclude with(Upon receipt of payment) the following developments toward a successful Funeral Ceremony Certification:

Phase (1) You will be given an Interview Checklist of a mock Scenario and from it; the following documents to submit:
(a) A Celebrant Ceremony Draft + an Anatomy Of Ceremony.
(b) A Client Ceremony Script.
(c) A video of your rehearsal(as you would present it). Appointments can be adjusted for one on one live grading and assistance with tutor(to play the others part in script). Interactive communications can take place, to answer any questions and exactly as it would be; when dealing with in real time and with clients(by calling them up to ask for any missing information).

WHERE DO WE GO FROM HERE ?

"The Advanced" package; to conclude with the following developments, for a successful Funeral Celebrant Certification:

Phase (2) A booking with a client for a ceremony.

After making contact with your client, the following considerations must be made:

(a) A copy of (after all revisions have been made) "The Celebrant Ceremony Script" and attached to it, with "The Anatomy Of a Ceremony".

(b) A copy as you would be giving to your client of "The Client Ceremony Script".

(c) Prior to the actual ceremony; a video copy of a well rehearsed ceremony.

(d) As soon as a booking is to take place and without any delay; (ASAP) contact us to VIP in a mentor.
To finalize a grade of accomplishment; distinctly sign your book and as you too will witness. The book will become your very own reference, at hand and you will be well on your way to the next "Stage of the process"
(if you so wish it)as a Family Celebrant with Volume 2.
(Volume 1 + Volume 2 = Diploma).

(e) You are to make a photo copy of the "Practical Evaluation and Examination Sheet".
Along with (a)+(b)+(c) submit to us for your final grade
And hurray, your certification will be on its way.

ACIFC   CSOC

Practical Evaluation and Examination Sheet:

(Include what day) Date: _____   Time Start :   Finish :

Name of Mentor _____ Sign _____

Name of Venue _____

Name of Student _____ Sign _____

CEREMONY TYPE: _____

TOTAL GRADE OF PERFORMANCE

_____

Public Speaking: _____ /25%

Voice Conduct   /10% Connection   /10% Confidence   /5%

Officiating: _____ /25%

Synergy   /6%   Synchronicity   /6%   Leadership   /13%

Content of Script: _____ /30%

Synergy   /10%   Synchronicity   /10%   Depth/Quality   /10%

Appearance: _____ /20%

Image Conduct   /10%   Self Esteem   /10%

canadiansocietyofcelebrantss@gmail.com

The Funeral Officiant & Ceremony